THE UNCANNY

X-MEN

™

TOR
®

A TOM DOHERTY ASSOCIATES BOOK
NEW YORK

This is a work of fiction. All the characters and events portrayed in this book are fictitious, and any resemblance to real people or events is purely coincidental.

THE UNCANNY X-MEN®

Originally published in magazine form as X-MEN #110, #123, and #124.

A Tor Book
Published by Tom Doherty Associates, Inc.
175 Fifth Ave.
New York, N.Y. 10010

ISBN: 0-812-51021-6

First printing: November 1990

Printed in the United States of America

0 9 8 7 6 5 4 3 2

The "X"-Sanction: *Chris Claremont, author; Tony De-Zuniga, artist; Annette Kawecki, letterer; Archie Goodwin, editor*

"Listen — Stop Me If You've Heard It — But This One Will **Kill** You!": *A Chris Claremont • John Byrne • Terry Austin Production; Tom Orz, letterer; Roger Stern, editor; Jim Shooter, editor-in-chief*

He Only Laughs When I Hurt!: *Chris Claremont, author; John Byrne, penciler; Chris Claremont & John Byrne, co-plotters; Terry Austin, inker; Tom Orzechowski, letterer; Roger Stern, editor; Jim Shooter, editor-in-chief*

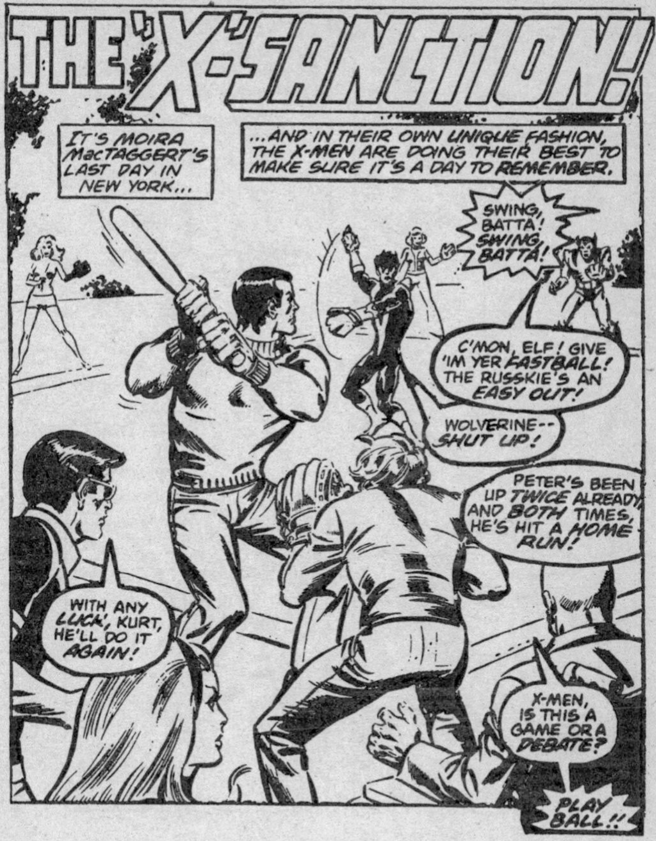
THE "X"-SANCTION!
IT'S MOIRA MacTAGGERT'S LAST DAY IN NEW YORK...
...AND IN THEIR OWN UNIQUE FASHION, THE X-MEN ARE DOING THEIR BEST TO MAKE SURE IT'S A DAY TO REMEMBER.
SWING, BATTA! SWING, BATTA!
C'MON, ELF! GIVE 'IM YER FASTBALL! THE RUSSKIE'S AN EASY OUT!
WOLVERINE-- SHUT UP!
PETER'S BEEN UP TWICE ALREADY, AND BOTH TIMES, HE'S HIT A HOME RUN!
WITH ANY LUCK, KURT, HE'LL DO IT AGAIN!
X-MEN, IS THIS A GAME OR A DEBATE?
PLAY BALL!!

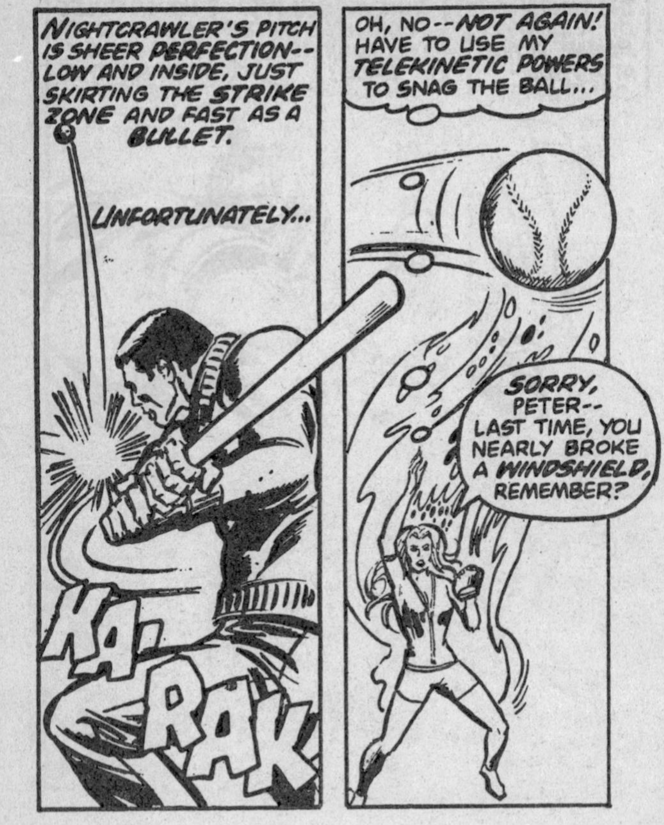
NIGHTCRAWLER'S PITCH IS SHEER PERFECTION-- LOW AND INSIDE, JUST SKIRTING THE STRIKE ZONE AND FAST AS A BULLET.
UNFORTUNATELY...
KA-RAK
OH, NO--NOT AGAIN! HAVE TO USE MY TELEKINETIC POWERS TO SNAG THE BALL...
SORRY, PETER-- LAST TIME, YOU NEARLY BROKE A WINDSHIELD, REMEMBER?

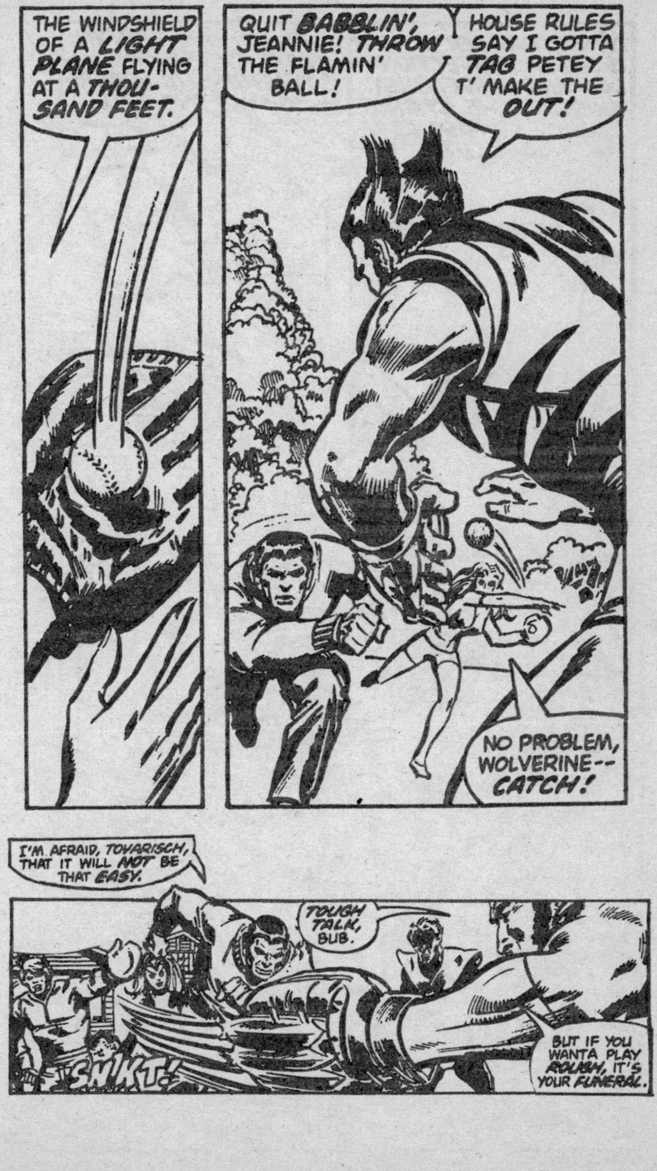
THE WINDSHIELD OF A LIGHT PLANE FLYING AT A THOU-SAND FEET.
QUIT BABBLIN', JEANNIE! THROW THE FLAMIN' BALL!
HOUSE RULES SAY I GOTTA TAG PETEY T' MAKE THE OUT!
NO PROBLEM, WOLVERINE--CATCH!
I'M AFRAID, TOVARISCH, THAT IT WILL NOT BE THAT EASY.
TOUGH TALK, BUB.
SNIKT!
BUT IF YOU WANTA PLAY ROUGH, IT'S YOUR FUNERAL.

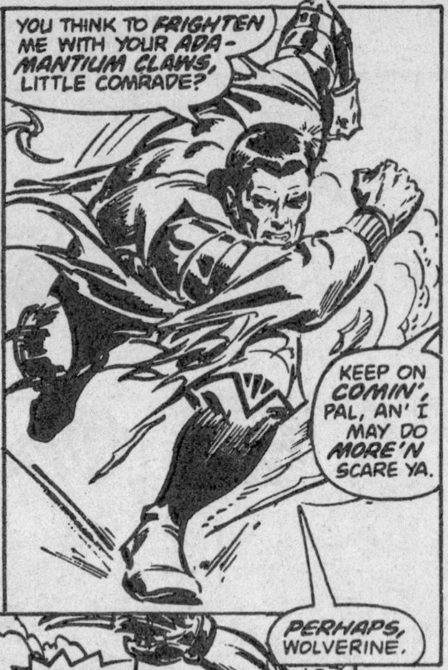
YOU THINK TO FRIGHTEN ME WITH YOUR ADAMANTIUM CLAWS, LITTLE COMRADE?
KEEP ON COMIN', PAL, AN' I MAY DO MORE'N SCARE YA.
PERHAPS, WOLVERINE.

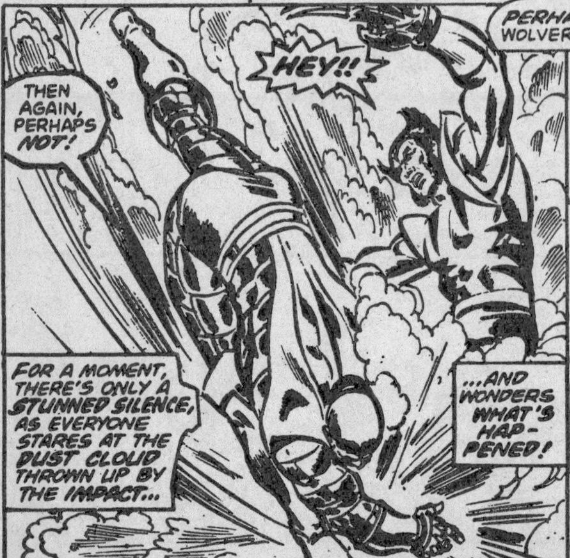
HEY!!
THEN AGAIN, PERHAPS NOT!
FOR A MOMENT, THERE'S ONLY A STUNNED SILENCE, AS EVERYONE STARES AT THE DUST CLOUD THROWN UP BY THE IMPACT...
...AND WONDERS WHAT'S HAPPENED!

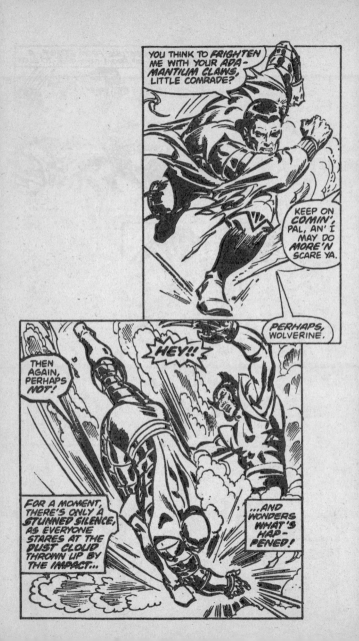

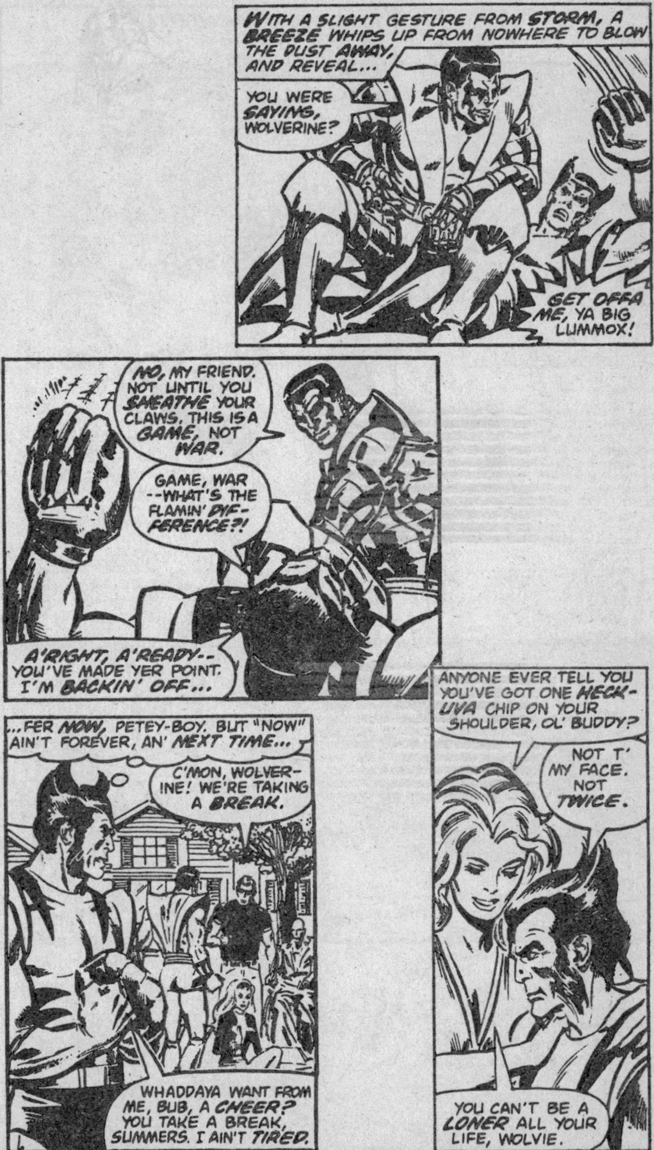
WITH A SLIGHT GESTURE FROM STORM, A BREEZE WHIPS UP FROM NOWHERE TO BLOW THE DUST AWAY, AND REVEAL...
YOU WERE SAYING, WOLVERINE?
GET OFFA ME, YA BIG LUMMOX!
NO, MY FRIEND. NOT UNTIL YOU SHEATHE YOUR CLAWS. THIS IS A GAME, NOT WAR.
GAME, WAR --WHAT'S THE FLAMIN' DIF-FERENCE?!
A'RIGHT, A'READY-- YOU'VE MADE YER POINT. I'M BACKIN' OFF...
...FER NOW, PETEY-BOY. BUT "NOW" AIN'T FOREVER, AN' NEXT TIME...
C'MON, WOLVER-INE! WE'RE TAKING A BREAK.
WHADDAYA WANT FROM ME, BUB, A CHEER? YOU TAKE A BREAK, SUMMERS. I AIN'T TIRED.
ANYONE EVER TELL YOU YOU'VE GOT ONE HECK-UVA CHIP ON YOUR SHOULDER, OL' BUDDY?
NOT T' MY FACE. NOT TWICE.
YOU CAN'T BE A LONER ALL YOUR LIFE, WOLVIE.

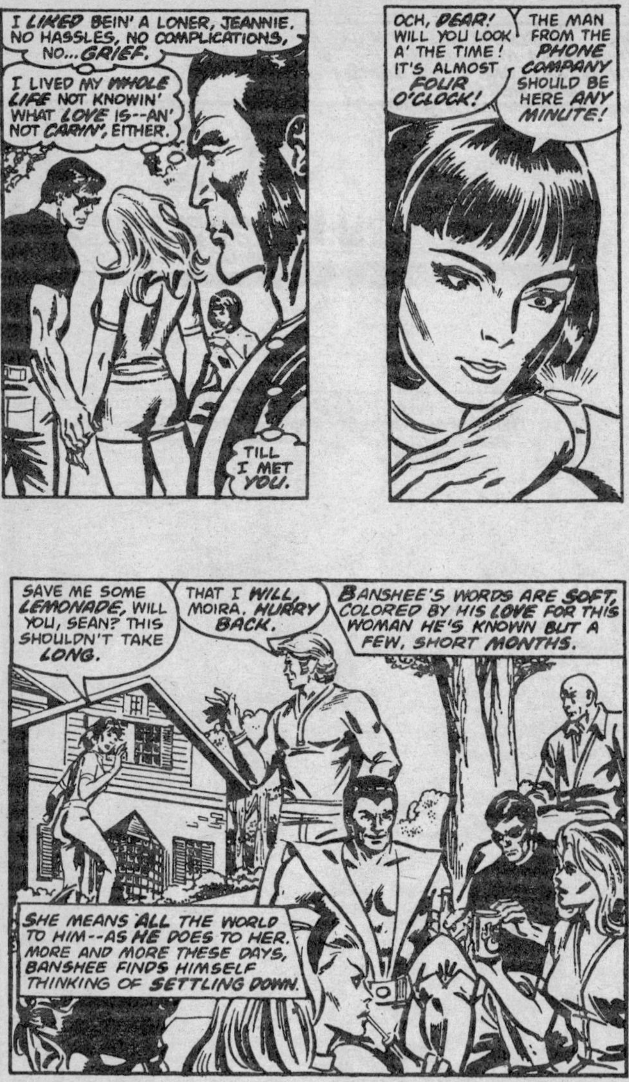

I LIKED BEIN' A LONER, JEANNIE. NO HASSLES, NO COMPLICATIONS, NO...GRIEF.
I LIVED MY WHOLE LIFE NOT KNOWIN' WHAT LOVE IS--AN' NOT CARIN', EITHER.
TILL I MET YOU.
OCH, DEAR! WILL YOU LOOK A' THE TIME! IT'S ALMOST FOUR O'CLOCK!
THE MAN FROM THE PHONE COMPANY SHOULD BE HERE ANY MINUTE!
SAVE ME SOME LEMONADE, WILL YOU, SEAN? THIS SHOULDN'T TAKE LONG.
THAT I WILL, MOIRA. HURRY BACK.
BANSHEE'S WORDS ARE SOFT, COLORED BY HIS LOVE FOR THIS WOMAN HE'S KNOWN BUT A FEW, SHORT MONTHS.
SHE MEANS ALL THE WORLD TO HIM--AS HE DOES TO HER. MORE AND MORE THESE DAYS, BANSHEE FINDS HIMSELF THINKING OF SETTLING DOWN.

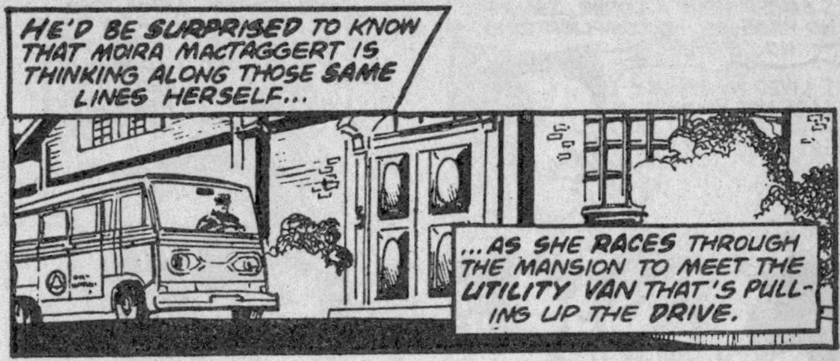
HE'D BE SURPRISED TO KNOW THAT MOIRA MACTAGGERT IS THINKING ALONG THOSE SAME LINES HERSELF...
...AS SHE RACES THROUGH THE MANSION TO MEET THE UTILITY VAN THAT'S PULLING UP THE DRIVE.

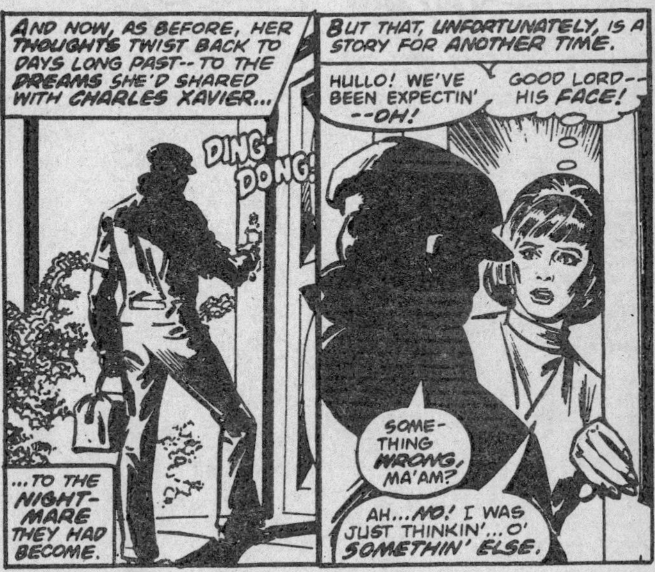
AND NOW, AS BEFORE, HER THOUGHTS TWIST BACK TO DAYS LONG PAST--TO THE DREAMS SHE'D SHARED WITH CHARLES XAVIER...
DING-DONG!
...TO THE NIGHTMARE THEY HAD BECOME.
BUT THAT, UNFORTUNATELY, IS A STORY FOR ANOTHER TIME.
HULLO! WE'VE BEEN EXPECTIN' --OH!
GOOD LORD--HIS FACE!
SOMETHING WRONG, MA'AM?
AH...NO! I WAS JUST THINKIN'...O' SOMETHIN' ELSE.

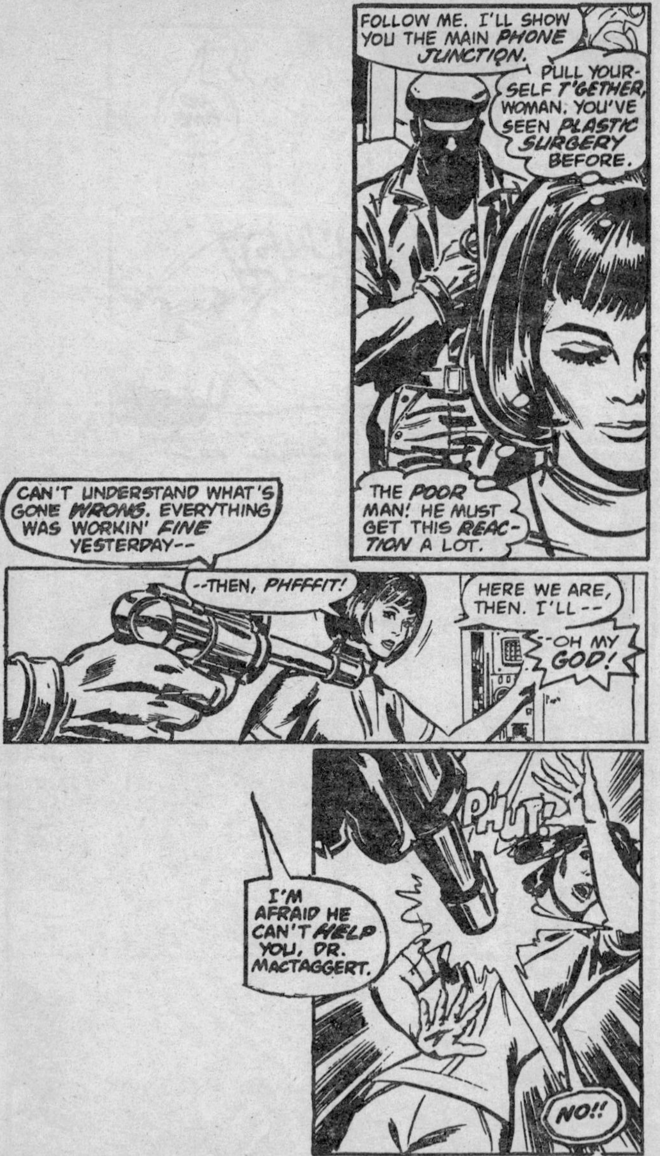
FOLLOW ME. I'LL SHOW YOU THE MAIN PHONE JUNCTION.
PULL YOURSELF T'GETHER, WOMAN. YOU'VE SEEN PLASTIC SURGERY BEFORE.
THE POOR MAN! HE MUST GET THIS REACTION A LOT.
CAN'T UNDERSTAND WHAT'S GONE WRONG. EVERYTHING WAS WORKIN' FINE YESTERDAY--
--THEN, PHFFFIT!
HERE WE ARE, THEN. I'LL--
--OH MY GOD!
PHUT!
I'M AFRAID HE CAN'T HELP YOU, DR. MACTAGGERT.
NO!!

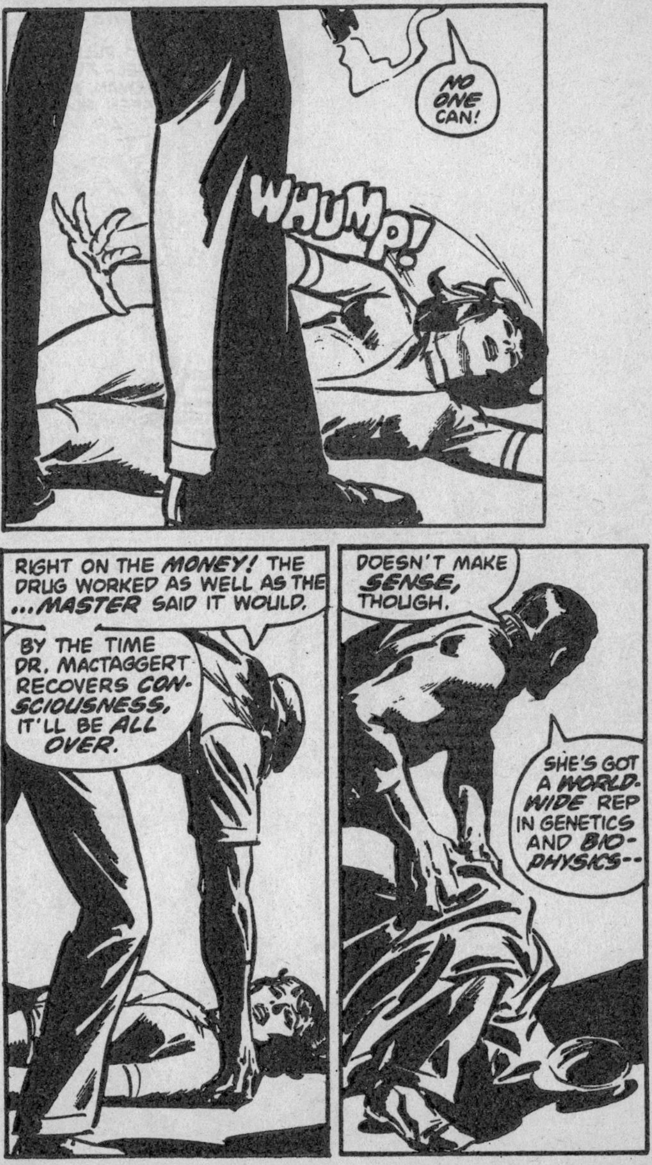
NO ONE CAN!
WHUMP!
RIGHT ON THE MONEY! THE DRUG WORKED AS WELL AS THE ...MASTER SAID IT WOULD.
BY THE TIME DR. MACTAGGERT RECOVERS CON-SCIOUSNESS, IT'LL BE ALL OVER.
DOESN'T MAKE SENSE, THOUGH.
SHE'S GOT A WORLD-WIDE REP IN GENETICS AND BIO-PHYSICS--

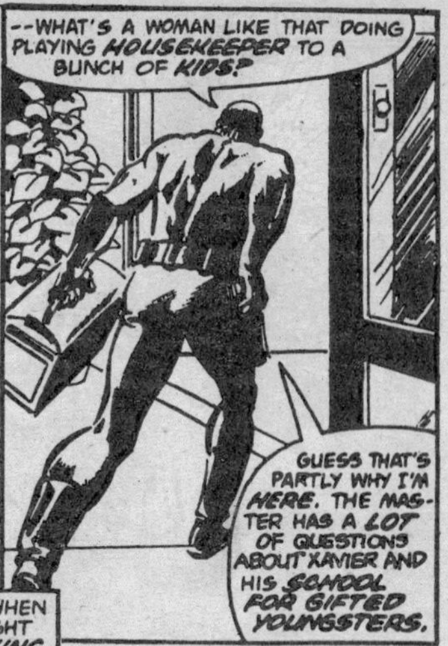
--WHAT'S A WOMAN LIKE THAT DOING PLAYING HOUSEKEEPER TO A BUNCH OF KIDS?
GUESS THAT'S PARTLY WHY I'M HERE. THE MASTER HAS A LOT OF QUESTIONS ABOUT XAVIER AND HIS SCHOOL FOR GIFTED YOUNGSTERS.

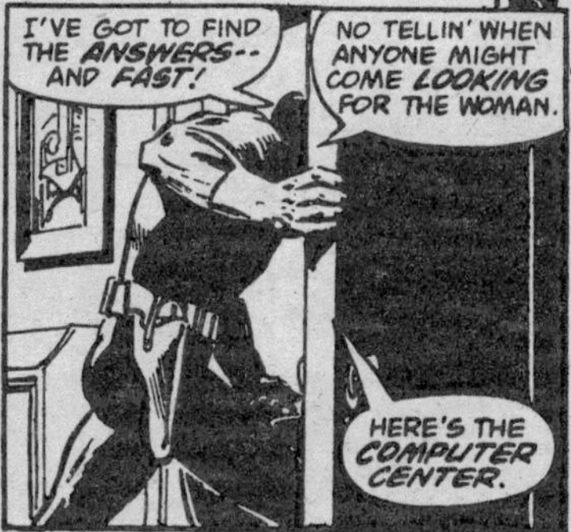
I'VE GOT TO FIND THE ANSWERS--AND FAST!
NO TELLIN' WHEN ANYONE MIGHT COME LOOKING FOR THE WOMAN.
HERE'S THE COMPUTER CENTER.

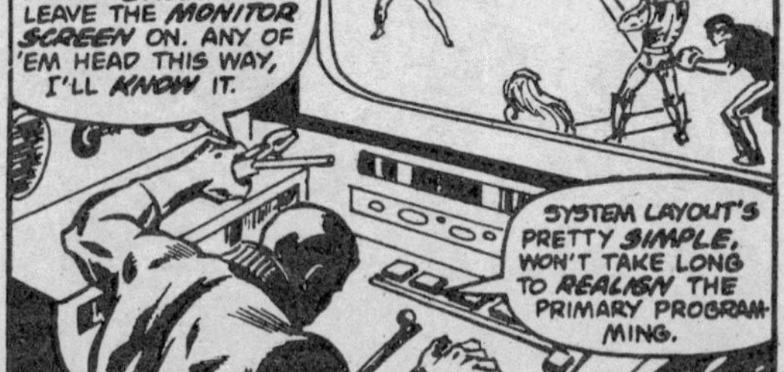
SO FAR, SO GOOD. EVERYONE'S OUT PLAYIN' BALL. I'LL LEAVE THE MONITOR SCREEN ON. ANY OF 'EM HEAD THIS WAY, I'LL KNOW IT.
SYSTEM LAYOUT'S PRETTY SIMPLE, WON'T TAKE LONG TO REALISIN THE PRIMARY PROGRAMMING.

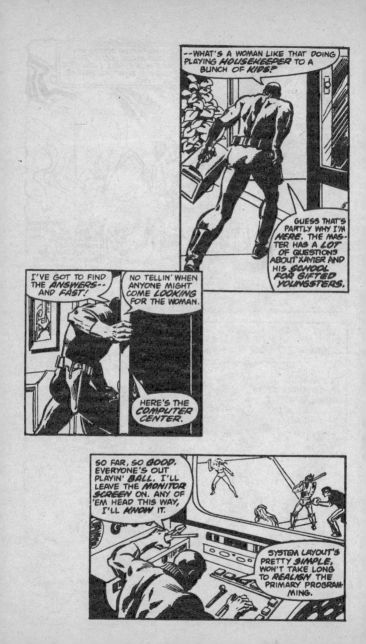

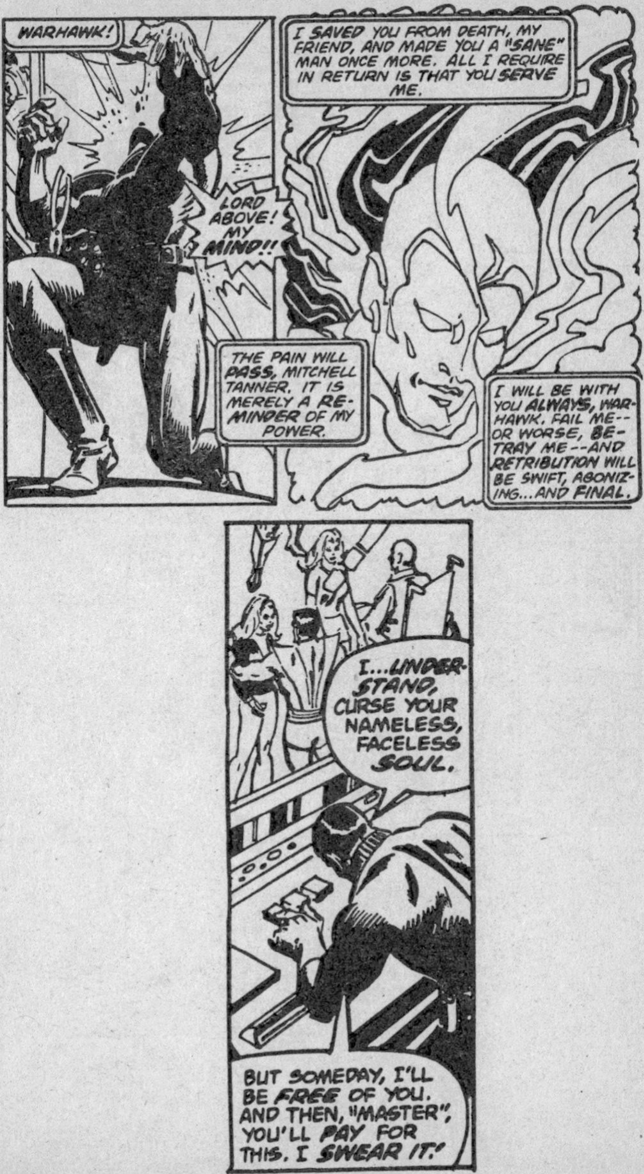
WARHAWK!
LORD ABOVE! MY MIND!!
THE PAIN WILL PASS, MITCHELL TANNER. IT IS MERELY A REMINDER OF MY POWER.
I SAVED YOU FROM DEATH, MY FRIEND, AND MADE YOU A "SANE" MAN ONCE MORE. ALL I REQUIRE IN RETURN IS THAT YOU SERVE ME.
I WILL BE WITH YOU ALWAYS, WARHAWK. FAIL ME--OR WORSE, BETRAY ME--AND RETRIBUTION WILL BE SWIFT, AGONIZING...AND FINAL.
I...UNDERSTAND, CURSE YOUR NAMELESS, FACELESS SOUL.
BUT SOMEDAY, I'LL BE FREE OF YOU. AND THEN, "MASTER", YOU'LL PAY FOR THIS. I SWEAR IT!

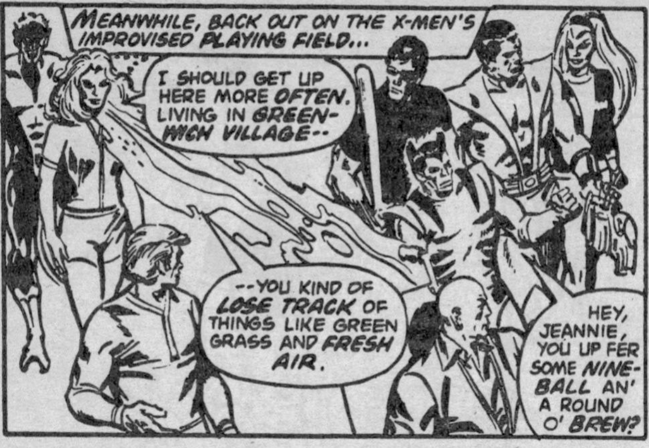
MEANWHILE, BACK OUT ON THE X-MEN'S IMPROVISED PLAYING FIELD...
I SHOULD GET UP HERE MORE OFTEN. LIVING IN GREEN-WICH VILLAGE--
--YOU KIND OF LOSE TRACK OF THINGS LIKE GREEN GRASS AND FRESH AIR.
HEY, JEANNIE, YOU UP FER SOME NINE-BALL AN' A ROUND O' BREW?

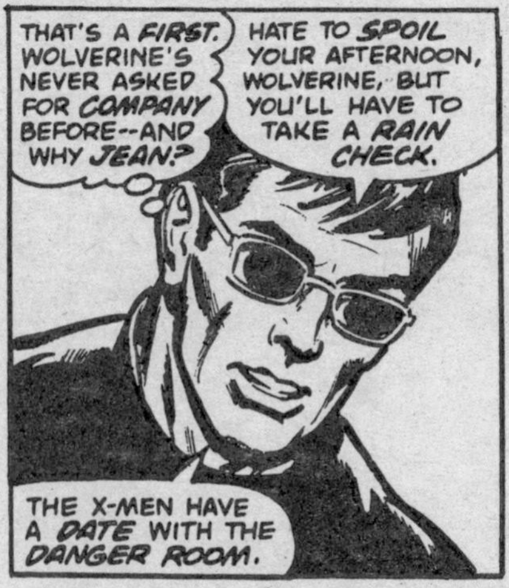
THAT'S A FIRST. WOLVERINE'S NEVER ASKED FOR COMPANY BEFORE--AND WHY JEAN?
HATE TO SPOIL YOUR AFTERNOON, WOLVERINE, BUT YOU'LL HAVE TO TAKE A RAIN CHECK.
THE X-MEN HAVE A DATE WITH THE DANGER ROOM.

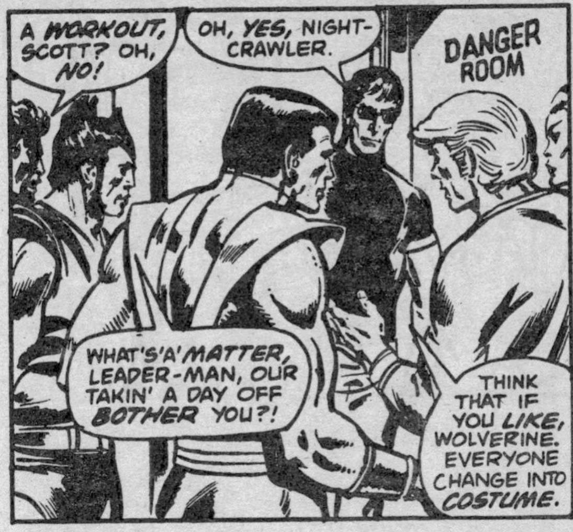

A WORKOUT, SCOTT? OH, NO!
OH, YES, NIGHT-CRAWLER.
DANGER ROOM
WHAT'S'A' MATTER, LEADER-MAN, OUR TAKIN' A DAY OFF BOTHER YOU?!
THINK THAT IF YOU LIKE, WOLVERINE. EVERYONE CHANGE INTO COSTUME.

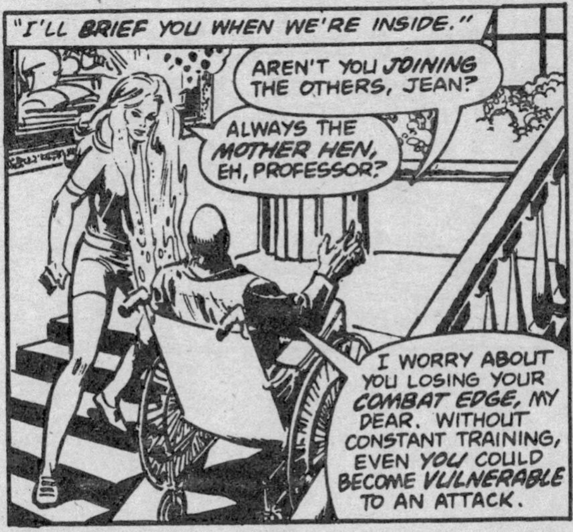

"I'LL BRIEF YOU WHEN WE'RE INSIDE."
AREN'T YOU JOINING THE OTHERS, JEAN?
ALWAYS THE MOTHER HEN, EH, PROFESSOR?
I WORRY ABOUT YOU LOSING YOUR COMBAT EDGE, MY DEAR. WITHOUT CONSTANT TRAINING, EVEN YOU COULD BECOME VULNERABLE TO AN ATTACK.

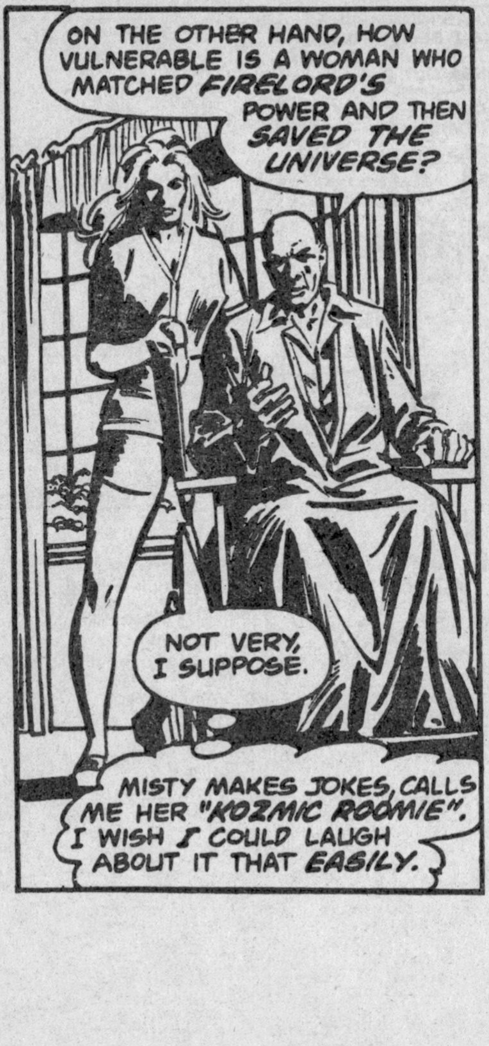
ON THE OTHER HAND, HOW VULNERABLE IS A WOMAN WHO MATCHED FIRELORD'S POWER AND THEN SAVED THE UNIVERSE?
NOT VERY, I SUPPOSE.
MISTY MAKES JOKES, CALLS ME HER "KOZMIC ROOMIE". I WISH I COULD LAUGH ABOUT IT THAT EASILY.

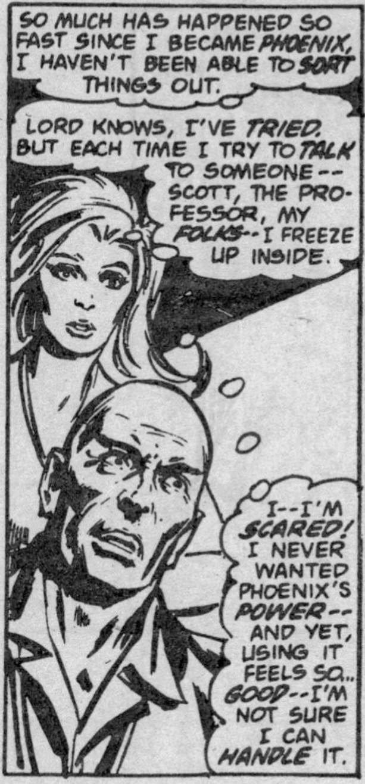
SO MUCH HAS HAPPENED SO FAST SINCE I BECAME PHOENIX, I HAVEN'T BEEN ABLE TO SORT THINGS OUT.
LORD KNOWS, I'VE TRIED. BUT EACH TIME I TRY TO TALK TO SOMEONE--SCOTT, THE PROFESSOR, MY FOLKS--I FREEZE UP INSIDE.
I--I'M SCARED! I NEVER WANTED PHOENIX'S POWER--AND YET, USING IT FEELS SO... GOOD--I'M NOT SURE I CAN HANDLE IT.

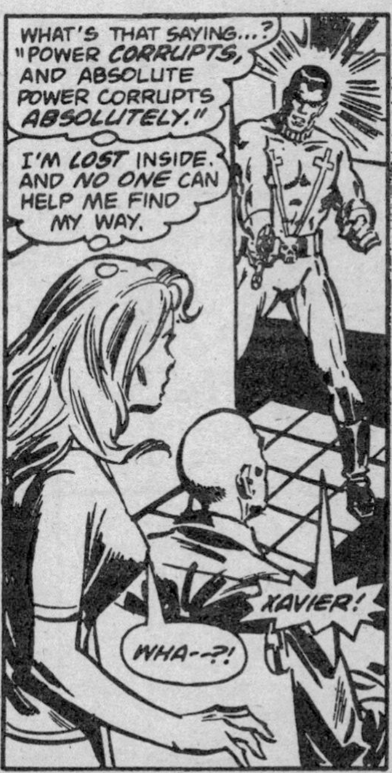
WHAT'S THAT SAYING...? "POWER CORRUPTS, AND ABSOLUTE POWER CORRUPTS ABSOLUTELY."
I'M LOST INSIDE. AND NO ONE CAN HELP ME FIND MY WAY.
XAVIER!
WHA--?!

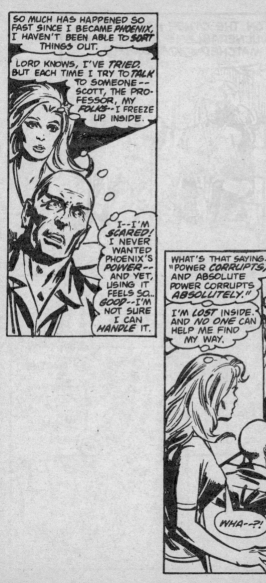

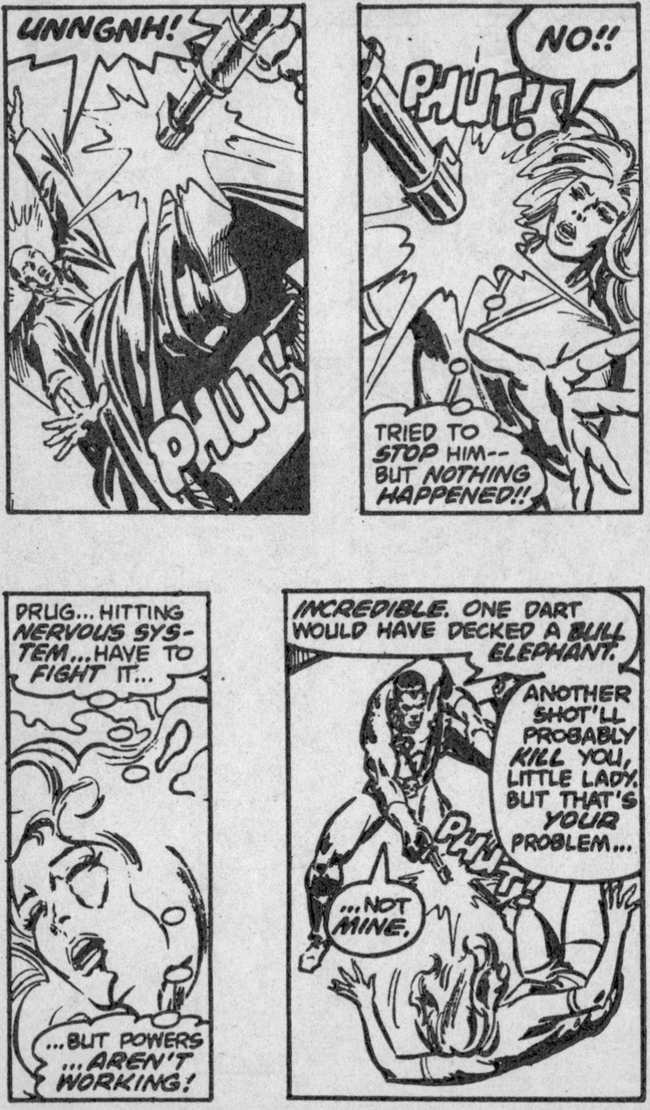
UNNGNH!
PHUT!
NO!!
PHUT!
TRIED TO STOP HIM-- BUT NOTHING HAPPENED!!
DRUG... HITTING NERVOUS SYS-TEM... HAVE TO FIGHT IT...
...BUT POWERS ...AREN'T WORKING!
INCREDIBLE. ONE DART WOULD HAVE DECKED A BULL ELEPHANT.
ANOTHER SHOT'LL PROBABLY KILL YOU, LITTLE LADY. BUT THAT'S YOUR PROBLEM...
PHUT!
...NOT MINE.

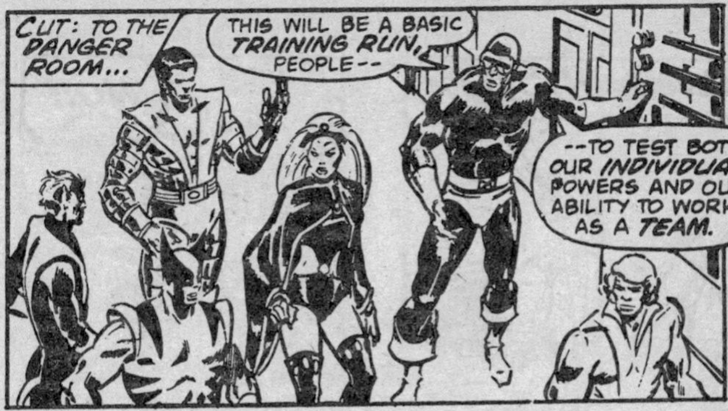
CUT: TO THE DANGER ROOM...
THIS WILL BE A BASIC TRAINING RUN, PEOPLE--
--TO TEST BOTH OUR INDIVIDUAL POWERS AND OUR ABILITY TO WORK AS A TEAM.

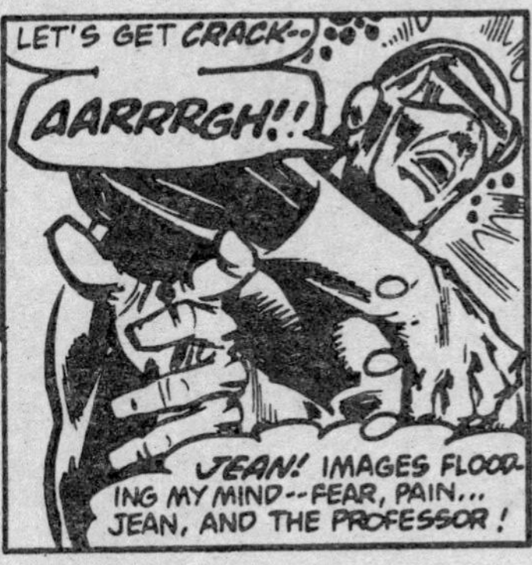
LET'S GET CRACK--
AARRRGH!!
JEAN! IMAGES FLOODING MY MIND--FEAR, PAIN... JEAN, AND THE PROFESSOR!

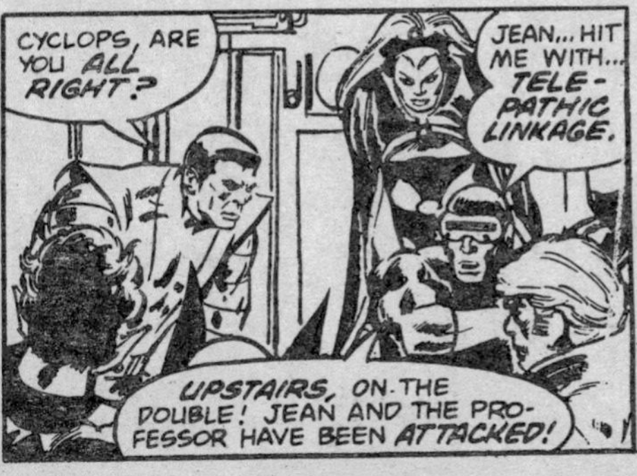
CYCLOPS, ARE YOU ALL RIGHT?
JEAN... HIT ME WITH... TELE-PATHIC LINKAGE.
UPSTAIRS, ON THE DOUBLE! JEAN AND THE PROFESSOR HAVE BEEN ATTACKED!

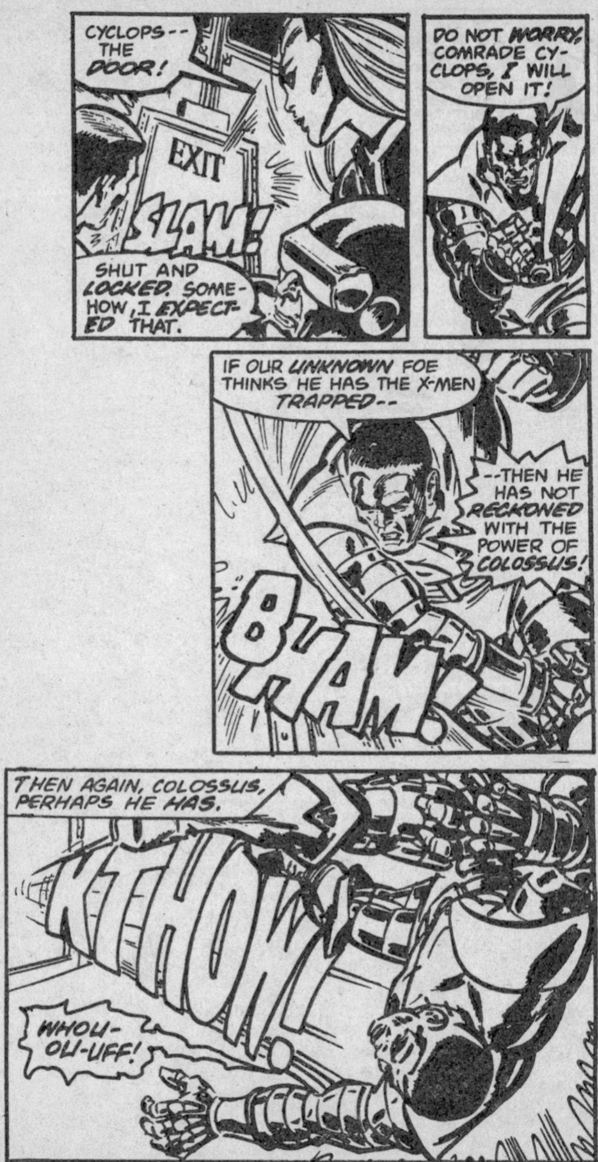
CYCLOPS-- THE DOOR!
SLAM!
SHUT AND LOCKED. SOMEHOW, I EXPECTED THAT.
DO NOT WORRY, COMRADE CYCLOPS, I WILL OPEN IT!
IF OUR UNKNOWN FOE THINKS HE HAS THE X-MEN TRAPPED--
--THEN HE HAS NOT RECKONED WITH THE POWER OF COLOSSUS!
BLAM!
THEN AGAIN, COLOSSUS, PERHAPS HE HAS.
KTHOW!
WHOU-OU-UFF!

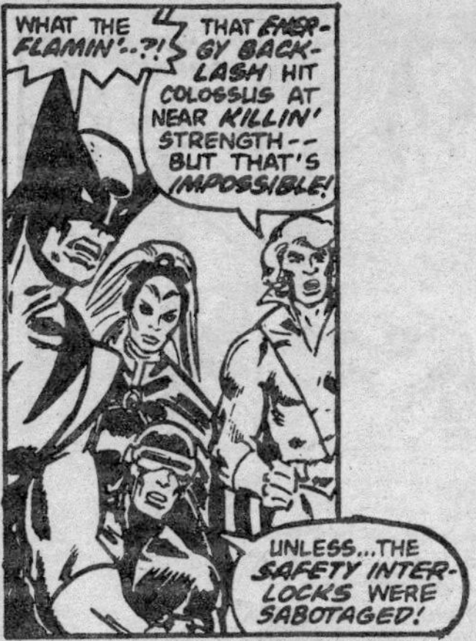
WHAT THE FLAMIN'..?!
THAT ENERGY BACKLASH HIT COLOSSUS AT NEAR KILLIN' STRENGTH-- BUT THAT'S IMPOSSIBLE!
UNLESS...THE SAFETY INTERLOCKS WERE SABOTAGED!

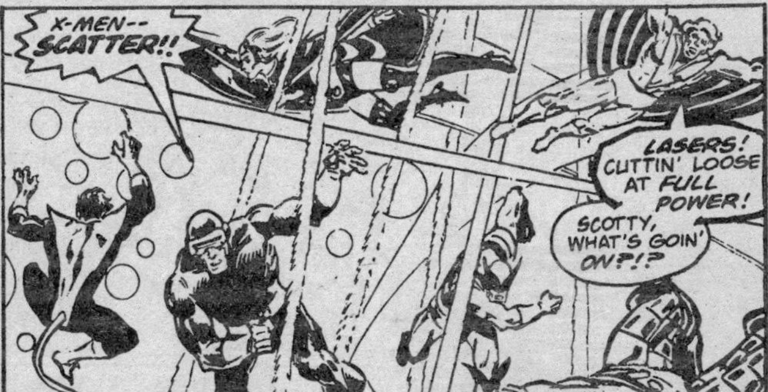
X-MEN-- SCATTER!!
LASERS! CUTTIN' LOOSE AT FULL POWER!
SCOTTY, WHAT'S GOIN' ON?!?

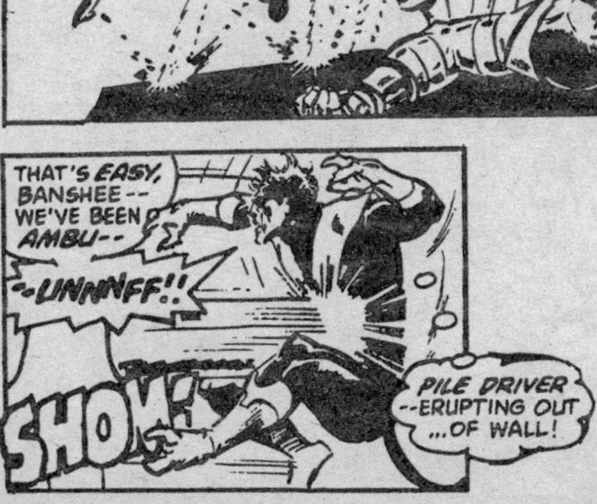
THAT'S EASY, BANSHEE-- WE'VE BEEN AMBU--
--UNNNFF!!
SHOOM!
PILE DRIVER --ERUPTING OUT ...OF WALL!

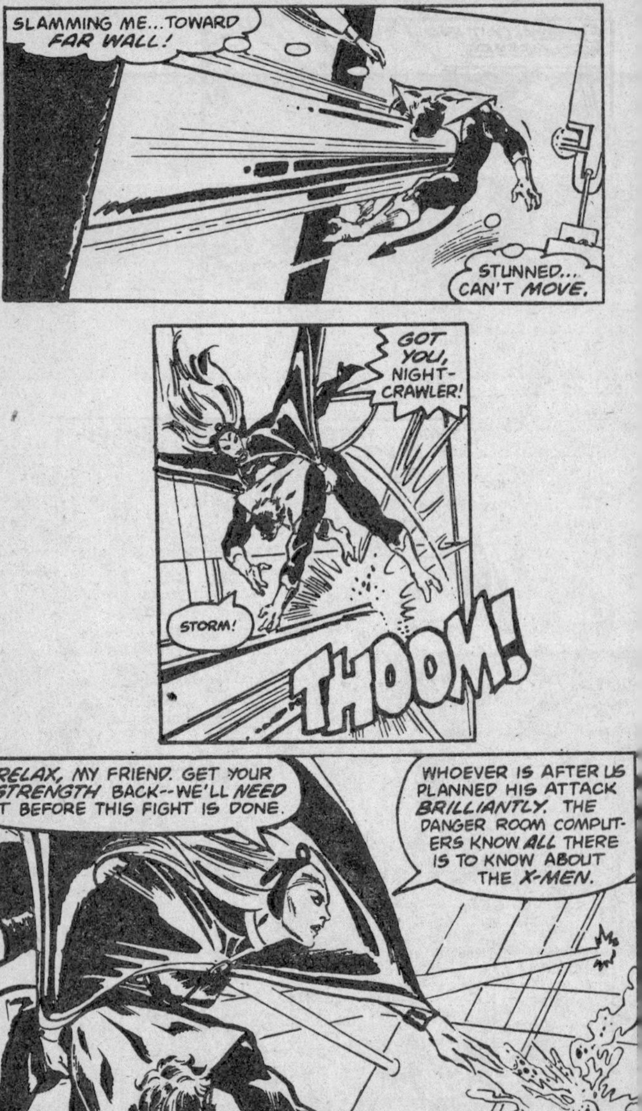

SLAMMING ME...TOWARD FAR WALL!
STUNNED... CAN'T MOVE.
GOT YOU, NIGHT-CRAWLER!
STORM!
THOOM!
RELAX, MY FRIEND. GET YOUR STRENGTH BACK--WE'LL NEED IT BEFORE THIS FIGHT IS DONE.
WHOEVER IS AFTER US PLANNED HIS ATTACK BRILLIANTLY. THE DANGER ROOM COMPUTERS KNOW ALL THERE IS TO KNOW ABOUT THE X-MEN.

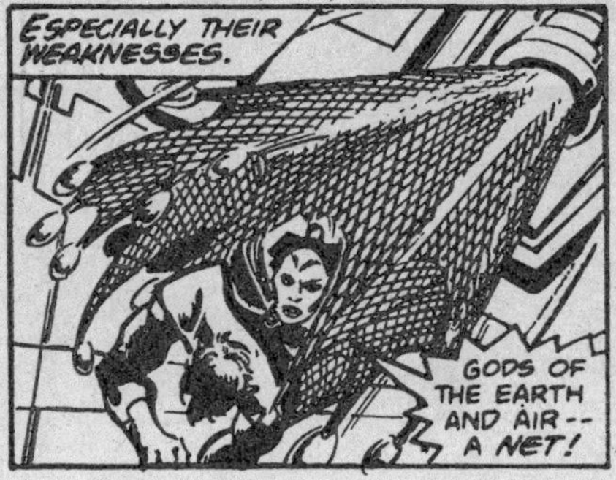
ESPECIALLY THEIR WEAKNESSES.
GODS OF THE EARTH AND AIR -- A NET!

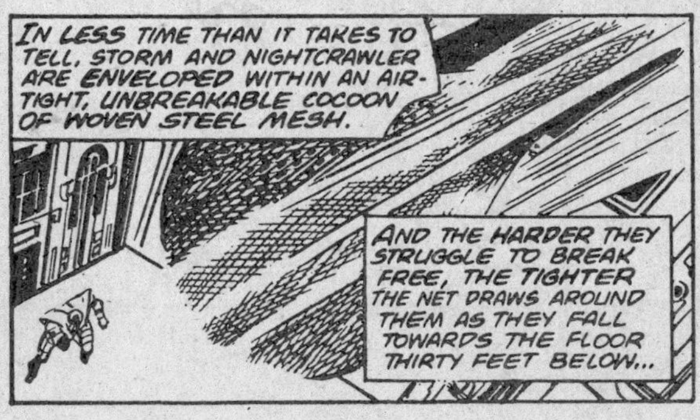
IN LESS TIME THAN IT TAKES TO TELL, STORM AND NIGHTCRAWLER ARE ENVELOPED WITHIN AN AIR-TIGHT, UNBREAKABLE COCOON OF WOVEN STEEL MESH.
AND THE HARDER THEY STRUGGLE TO BREAK FREE, THE TIGHTER THE NET DRAWS AROUND THEM AS THEY FALL TOWARDS THE FLOOR THIRTY FEET BELOW...

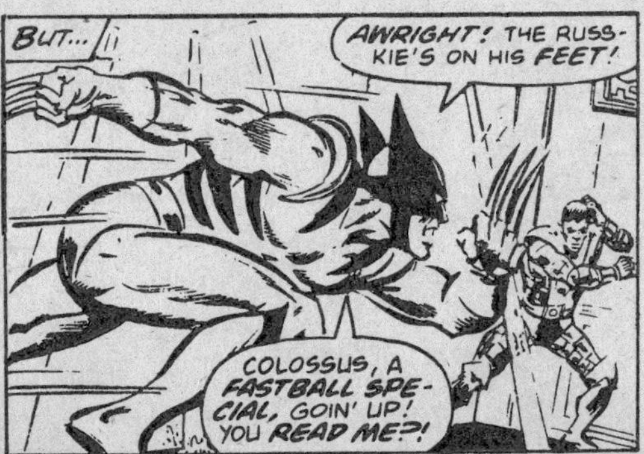
BUT...
AWRIGHT! THE RUSS-KIE'S ON HIS FEET!
COLOSSUS, A FASTBALL SPE-CIAL, GOIN' UP! YOU READ ME?!

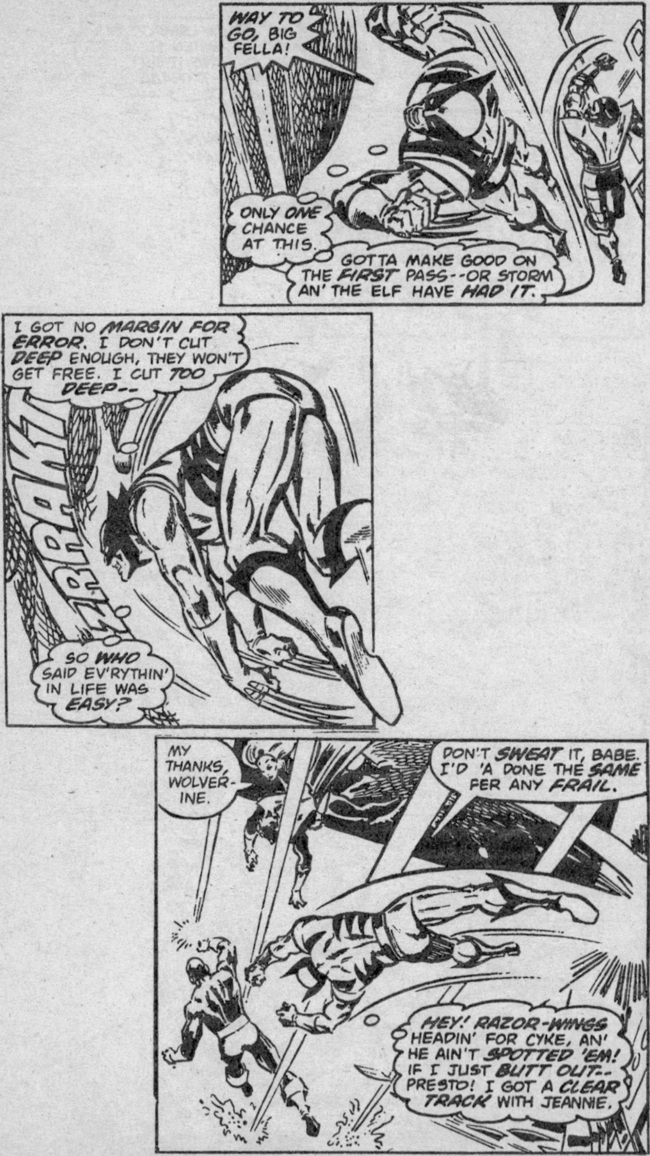
WAY TO GO, BIG FELLA!
ONLY ONE CHANCE AT THIS.
GOTTA MAKE GOOD ON THE FIRST PASS--OR STORM AN' THE ELF HAVE HAD IT.
I GOT NO MARGIN FOR ERROR. I DON'T CUT DEEP ENOUGH, THEY WON'T GET FREE. I CUT TOO DEEP--
SO WHO SAID EV'RYTHIN' IN LIFE WAS EASY?
MY THANKS, WOLVERINE.
DON'T SWEAT IT, BABE. I'D 'A DONE THE SAME FER ANY FRAIL.
HEY! RAZOR-WINGS HEADIN' FOR CYKE, AN' HE AIN'T SPOTTED 'EM! IF I JUST BUTT OUT--PRESTO! I GOT A CLEAR TRACK WITH JEANNIE.

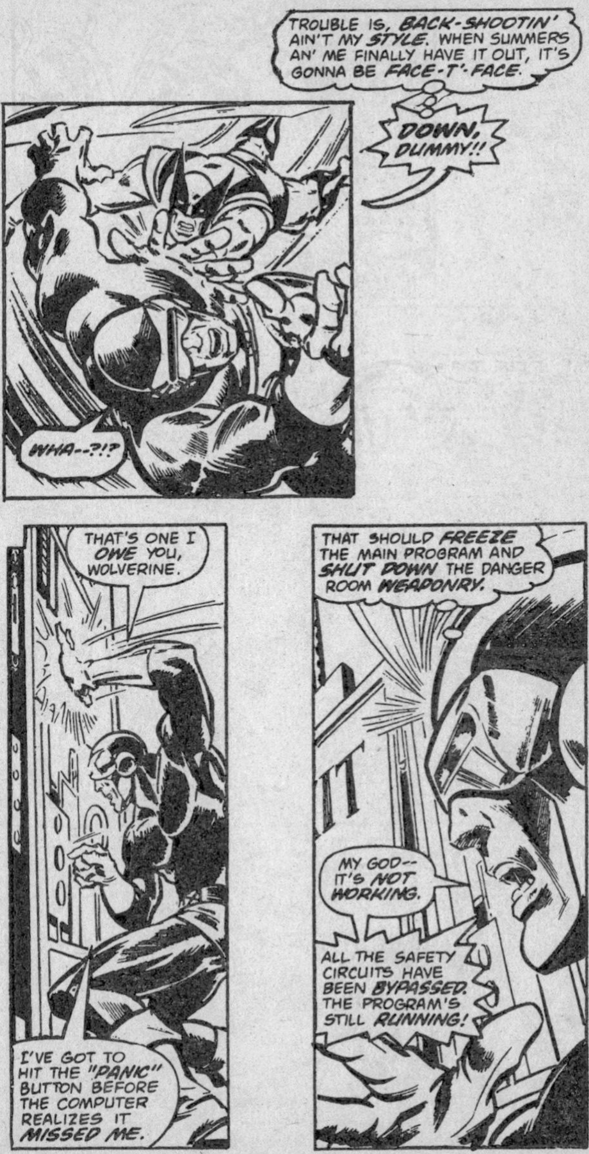
TROUBLE IS, BACK-SHOOTIN' AIN'T MY STYLE. WHEN SUMMERS AN' ME FINALLY HAVE IT OUT, IT'S GONNA BE FACE-T'-FACE.
DOWN, DUMMY!!
WHA--?!?
THAT'S ONE I OWE YOU, WOLVERINE.
I'VE GOT TO HIT THE "PANIC" BUTTON BEFORE THE COMPUTER REALIZES IT MISSED ME.
THAT SHOULD FREEZE THE MAIN PROGRAM AND SHUT DOWN THE DANGER ROOM WEAPONRY.
MY GOD-- IT'S NOT WORKING.
ALL THE SAFETY CIRCUITS HAVE BEEN BYPASSED. THE PROGRAM'S STILL RUNNING!

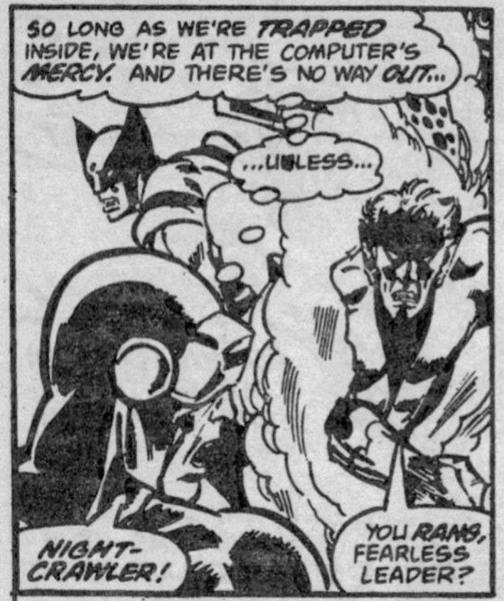
SO LONG AS WE'RE TRAPPED INSIDE, WE'RE AT THE COMPUTER'S MERCY. AND THERE'S NO WAY OUT...
...UNLESS...
NIGHT-CRAWLER!
YOU RANG, FEARLESS LEADER?

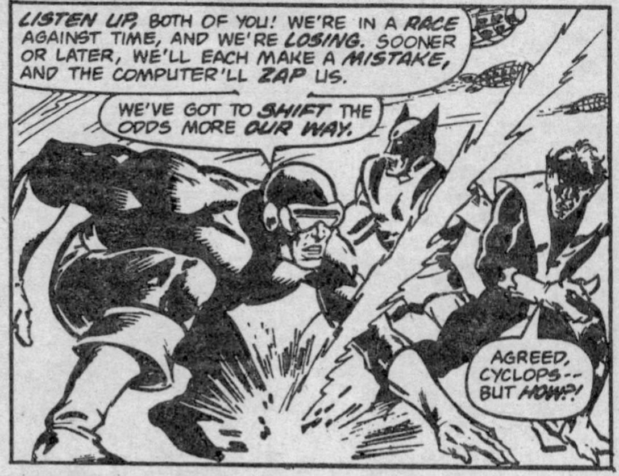
LISTEN UP, BOTH OF YOU! WE'RE IN A RACE AGAINST TIME, AND WE'RE LOSING. SOONER OR LATER, WE'LL EACH MAKE A MISTAKE, AND THE COMPUTER'LL ZAP US.
WE'VE GOT TO SHIFT THE ODDS MORE OUR WAY.
AGREED, CYCLOPS--BUT HOW?!

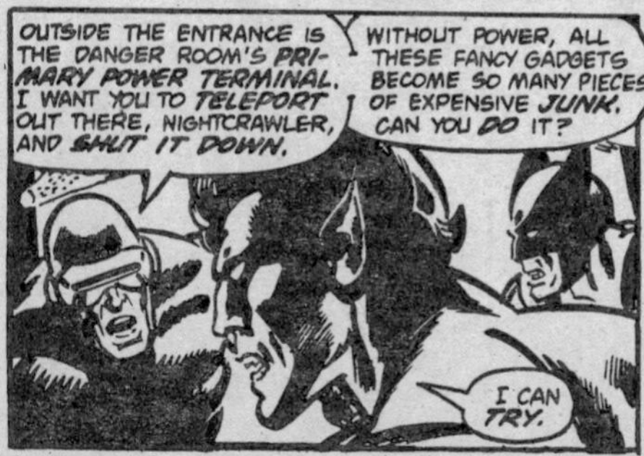
OUTSIDE THE ENTRANCE IS THE DANGER ROOM'S PRIMARY POWER TERMINAL. I WANT YOU TO TELEPORT OUT THERE, NIGHTCRAWLER, AND SHUT IT DOWN.
WITHOUT POWER, ALL THESE FANCY GADGETS BECOME SO MANY PIECES OF EXPENSIVE JUNK. CAN YOU DO IT?
I CAN TRY.

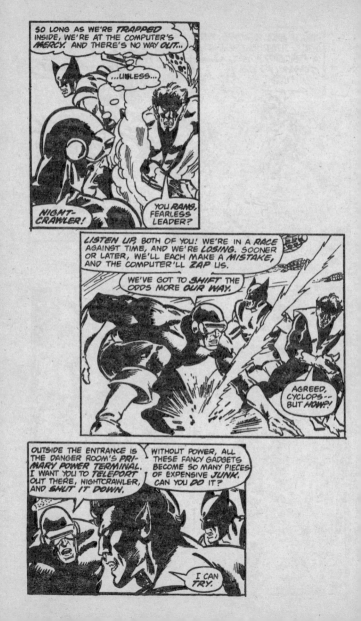

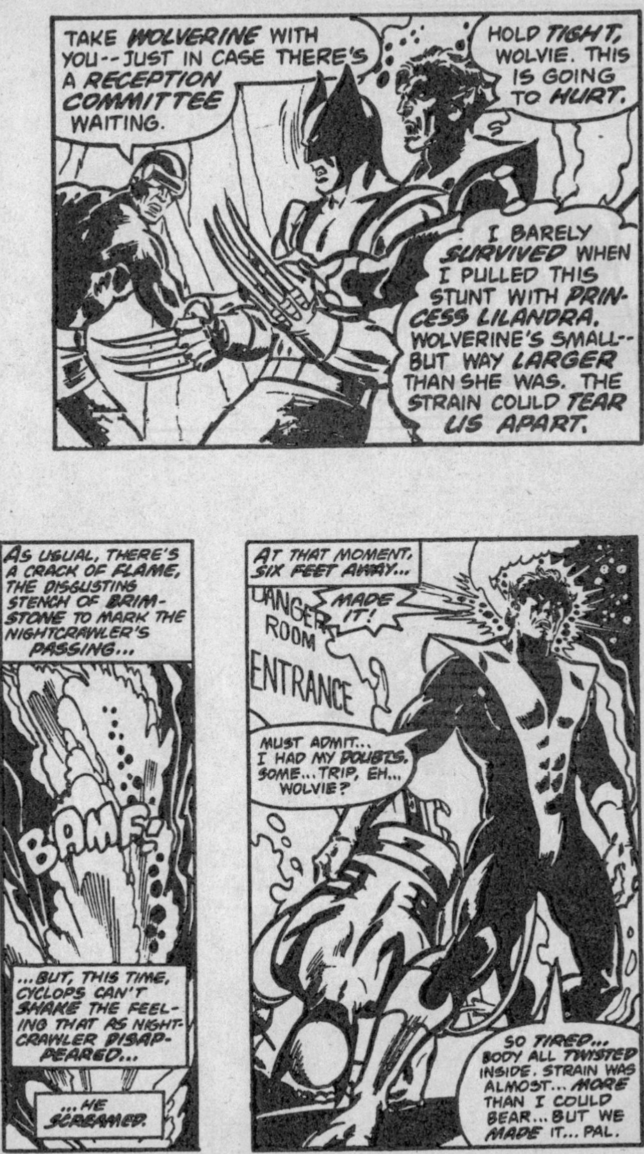
TAKE WOLVERINE WITH YOU--JUST IN CASE THERE'S A RECEPTION COMMITTEE WAITING.
HOLD TIGHT, WOLVIE. THIS IS GOING TO HURT.
I BARELY SURVIVED WHEN I PULLED THIS STUNT WITH PRINCESS LILANDRA. WOLVERINE'S SMALL--BUT WAY LARGER THAN SHE WAS. THE STRAIN COULD TEAR US APART.
AS USUAL, THERE'S A CRACK OF FLAME, THE DISGUSTING STENCH OF BRIMSTONE TO MARK THE NIGHTCRAWLER'S PASSING...
BAMF!
...BUT, THIS TIME, CYCLOPS CAN'T SHAKE THE FEELING THAT AS NIGHTCRAWLER DISAPPEARED...
...HE SCREAMED.
AT THAT MOMENT, SIX FEET AWAY...
DANGER ROOM ENTRANCE
MADE IT!
MUST ADMIT... I HAD MY DOUBTS. SOME...TRIP, EH... WOLVIE?
SO TIRED... BODY ALL TWISTED INSIDE. STRAIN WAS ALMOST... MORE THAN I COULD BEAR... BUT WE MADE IT... PAL.

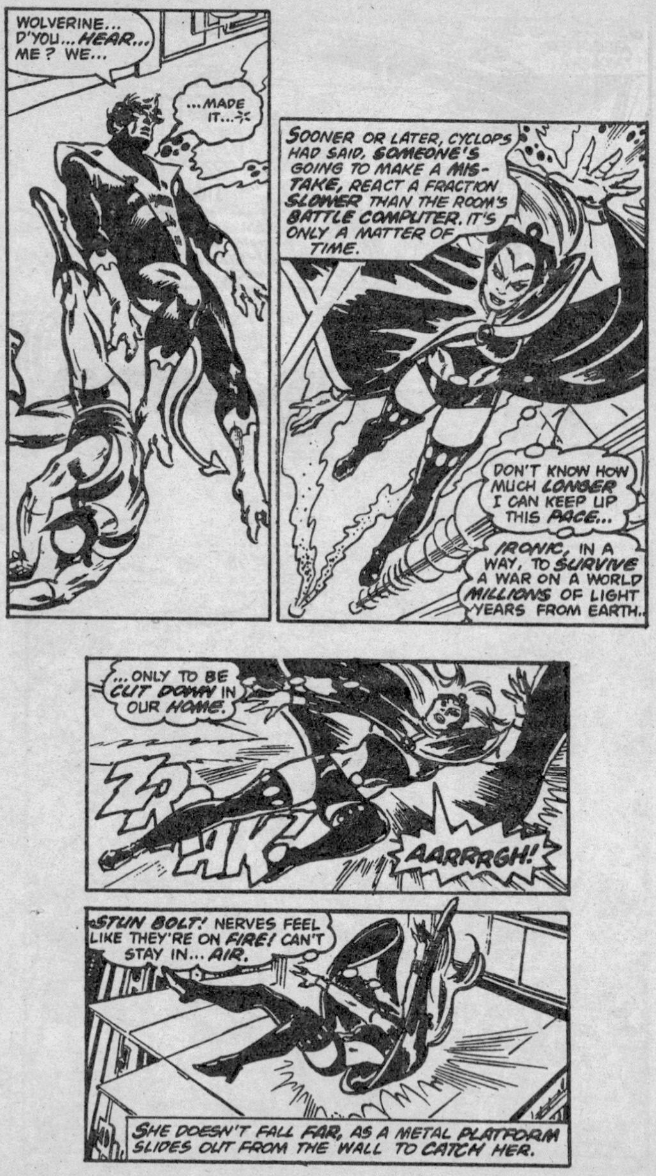

WOLVERINE... D'YOU... HEAR... ME? WE...
...MADE IT...
SOONER OR LATER, CYCLOPS HAD SAID, SOMEONE'S GOING TO MAKE A MISTAKE, REACT A FRACTION SLOWER THAN THE ROOM'S BATTLE COMPUTER. IT'S ONLY A MATTER OF TIME.
DON'T KNOW HOW MUCH LONGER I CAN KEEP UP THIS PACE...
IRONIC, IN A WAY, TO SURVIVE A WAR ON A WORLD MILLIONS OF LIGHT YEARS FROM EARTH..
...ONLY TO BE CUT DOWN IN OUR HOME.
ZRAK!
AARRRGH!
STUN BOLT! NERVES FEEL LIKE THEY'RE ON FIRE! CAN'T STAY IN... AIR.
SHE DOESN'T FALL FAR, AS A METAL PLATFORM SLIDES OUT FROM THE WALL TO CATCH HER.

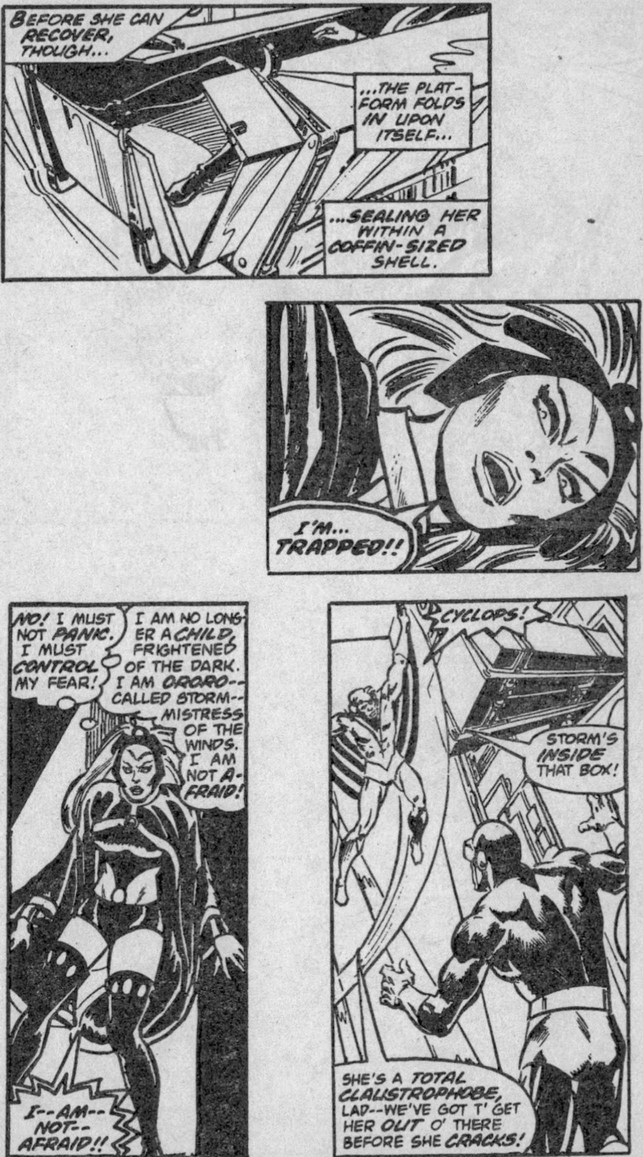
BEFORE SHE CAN RECOVER, THOUGH...
...THE PLATFORM FOLDS IN UPON ITSELF...
...SEALING HER WITHIN A COFFIN-SIZED SHELL.
I'M... TRAPPED!!
NO! I MUST NOT PANIC. I MUST CONTROL MY FEAR!
I AM NO LONGER A CHILD, FRIGHTENED OF THE DARK. I AM ORORO-- CALLED STORM-- MISTRESS OF THE WINDS. I AM NOT AFRAID!
I--AM--NOT--AFRAID!!
CYCLOPS!
STORM'S INSIDE THAT BOX!
SHE'S A TOTAL CLAUSTROPHOBE, LAD--WE'VE GOT T' GET HER OUT O' THERE BEFORE SHE CRACKS!

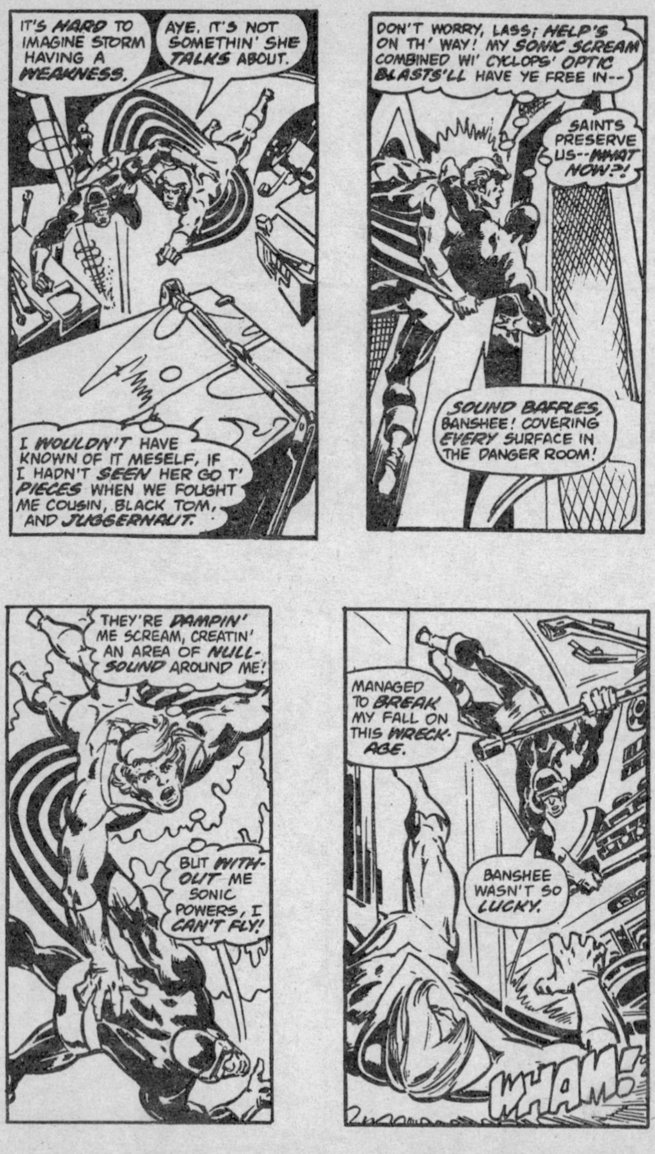
IT'S HARD TO IMAGINE STORM HAVING A WEAKNESS.
AYE. IT'S NOT SOMETHIN' SHE TALKS ABOUT.
I WOULDN'T HAVE KNOWN OF IT MESELF, IF I HADN'T SEEN HER GO T' PIECES WHEN WE FOUGHT ME COUSIN, BLACK TOM, AND JUGGERNAUT.
DON'T WORRY, LASS; HELP'S ON TH' WAY! MY SONIC SCREAM COMBINED WI' CYCLOPS' OPTIC BLASTS'LL HAVE YE FREE IN--
SAINTS PRESERVE US--WHAT NOW?!
SOUND BAFFLES, BANSHEE! COVERING EVERY SURFACE IN THE DANGER ROOM!
THEY'RE DAMPIN' ME SCREAM, CREATIN' AN AREA OF NULL-SOUND AROUND ME!
BUT WITH-OUT ME SONIC POWERS, I CAN'T FLY!
MANAGED TO BREAK MY FALL ON THIS WRECK-AGE.
BANSHEE WASN'T SO LUCKY.
WHAM!

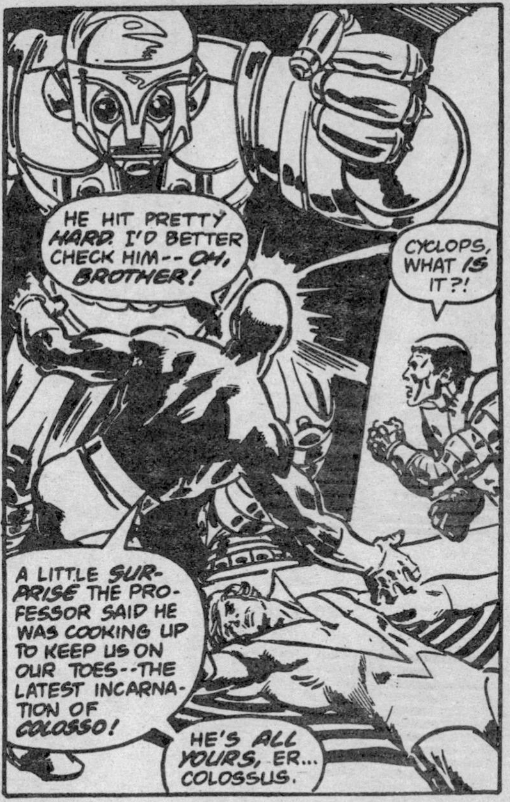
HE HIT PRETTY HARD. I'D BETTER CHECK HIM--OH, BROTHER!
CYCLOPS, WHAT IS IT?!
A LITTLE SURPRISE THE PROFESSOR SAID HE WAS COOKING UP TO KEEP US ON OUR TOES--THE LATEST INCARNATION OF COLOSSO!
HE'S ALL YOURS, ER... COLOSSUS.

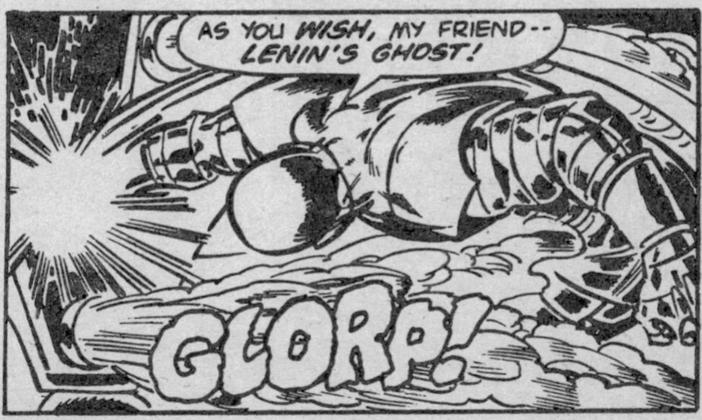
AS YOU WISH, MY FRIEND--LENIN'S GHOST!
GLORP!

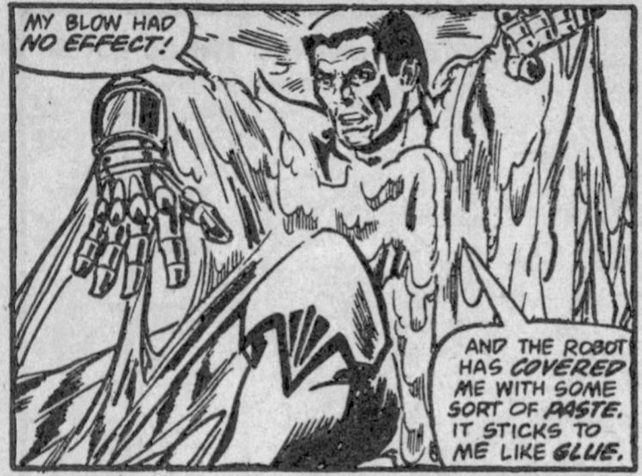
MY BLOW HAD NO EFFECT!
AND THE ROBOT HAS COVERED ME WITH SOME SORT OF PASTE. IT STICKS TO ME LIKE GLUE.

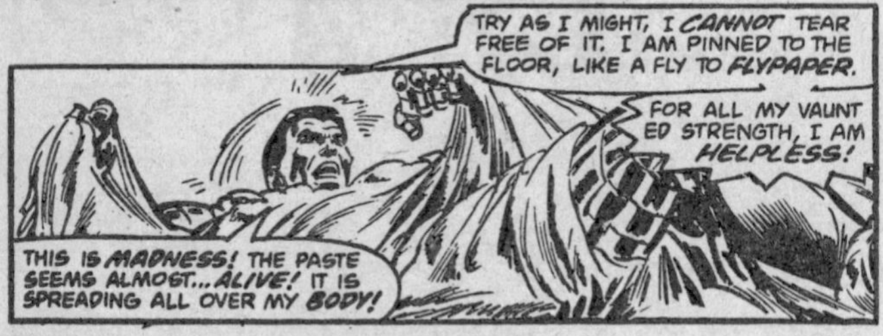
TRY AS I MIGHT, I CANNOT TEAR FREE OF IT. I AM PINNED TO THE FLOOR, LIKE A FLY TO FLYPAPER.
FOR ALL MY VAUNT ED STRENGTH, I AM HELPLESS!
THIS IS MADNESS! THE PASTE SEEMS ALMOST... ALIVE! IT IS SPREADING ALL OVER MY BODY!

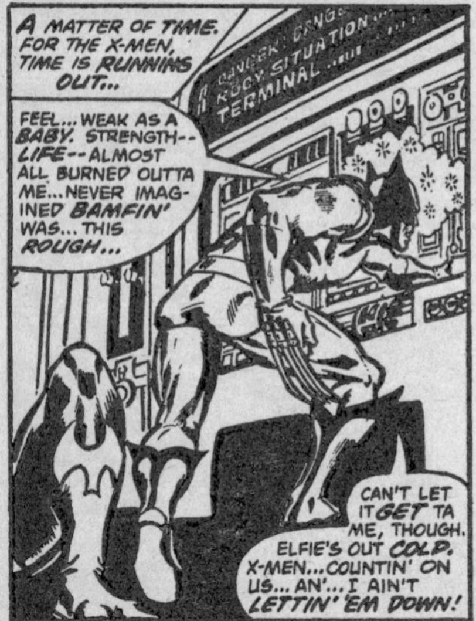
A MATTER OF TIME. FOR THE X-MEN, TIME IS RUNNING OUT...
FEEL... WEAK AS A BABY. STRENGTH-- LIFE-- ALMOST ALL BURNED OUTTA ME... NEVER IMAG-INED BAMFIN' WAS... THIS ROUGH...
CAN'T LET IT GET TA ME, THOUGH. ELFIE'S OUT COLD. X-MEN... COUNTIN' ON US... AN'... I AIN'T LETTIN' 'EM DOWN!

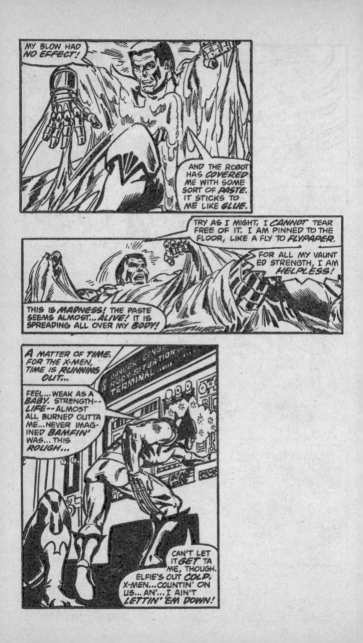

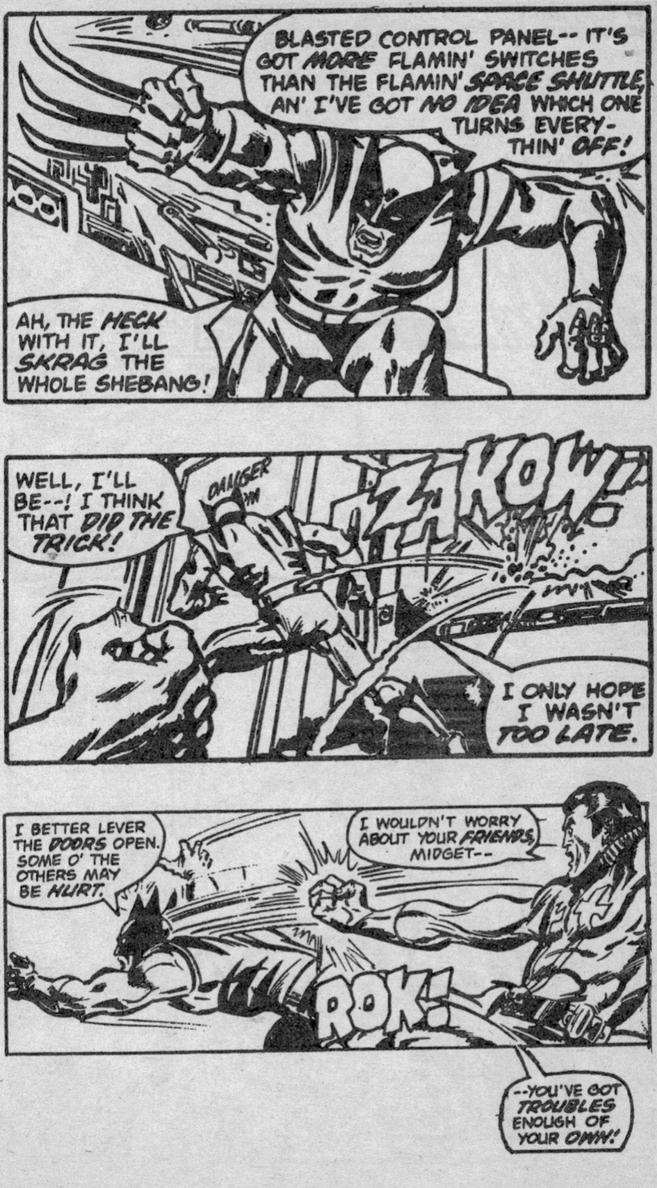
BLASTED CONTROL PANEL-- IT'S GOT *MORE* FLAMIN' SWITCHES THAN THE FLAMIN' *SPACE SHUTTLE*, AN' I'VE GOT *NO IDEA* WHICH ONE TURNS EVERY-THIN' *OFF*!
AH, THE *HECK* WITH IT, I'LL *SKRAG* THE WHOLE SHEBANG!
WELL, I'LL BE--! I THINK THAT *DID THE TRICK*!
ZAKOW!
I ONLY HOPE I WASN'T *TOO LATE*.
I BETTER LEVER THE *DOORS* OPEN. SOME O' THE OTHERS MAY BE *HURT*.
I WOULDN'T WORRY ABOUT YOUR *FRIENDS*, MIDGET--
ROK!
--YOU'VE GOT *TROUBLES* ENOUGH OF YOUR *OWN*!

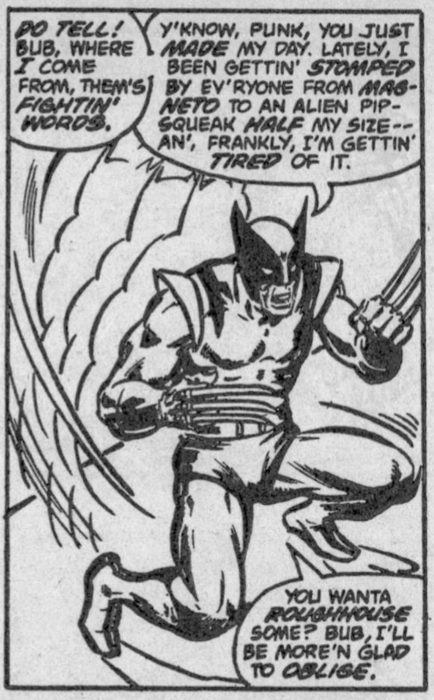
DO TELL! BUB, WHERE I COME FROM, THEM'S FIGHTIN' WORDS.
Y'KNOW, PUNK, YOU JUST MADE MY DAY. LATELY, I BEEN GETTIN' STOMPED BY EV'RYONE FROM MAGNETO TO AN ALIEN PIPSQUEAK HALF MY SIZE-- AN', FRANKLY, I'M GETTIN' TIRED OF IT.
YOU WANTA ROUGHHOUSE SOME? BUB, I'LL BE MORE'N GLAD TO OBLIGE.

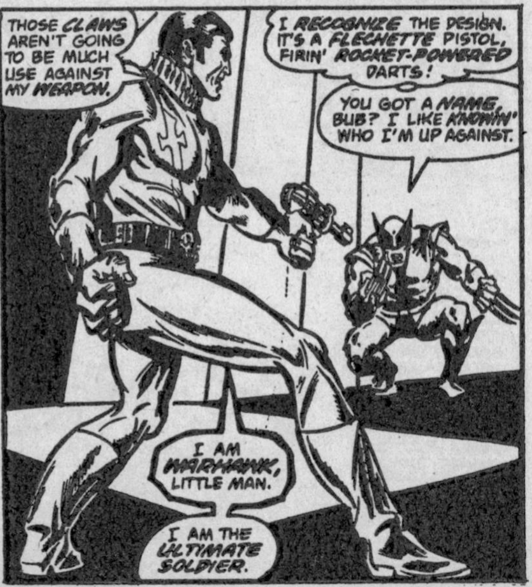
THOSE CLAWS AREN'T GOING TO BE MUCH USE AGAINST MY WEAPON.
I RECOGNIZE THE DESIGN. IT'S A FLECHETTE PISTOL, FIRIN' ROCKET-POWERED DARTS!
YOU GOT A NAME, BUB? I LIKE KNOWIN' WHO I'M UP AGAINST.
I AM WARHAWK, LITTLE MAN.
I AM THE ULTIMATE SOLDIER.

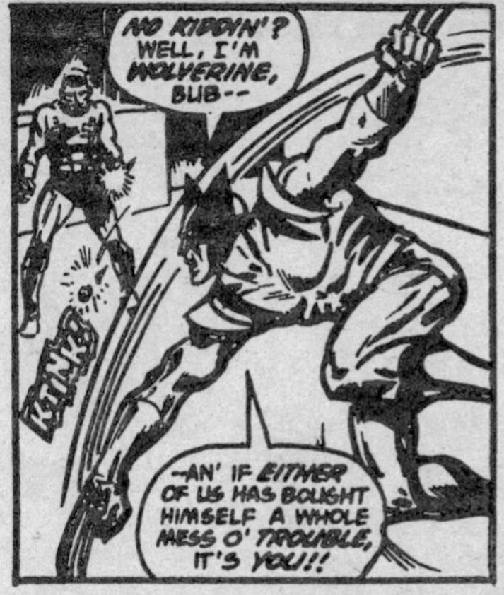
NO KIDDIN'? WELL, I'M WOLVERINE, BUB--
KTINK
--AN' IF EITHER OF US HAS BOUGHT HIMSELF A WHOLE MESS O' TROUBLE, IT'S YOU!!

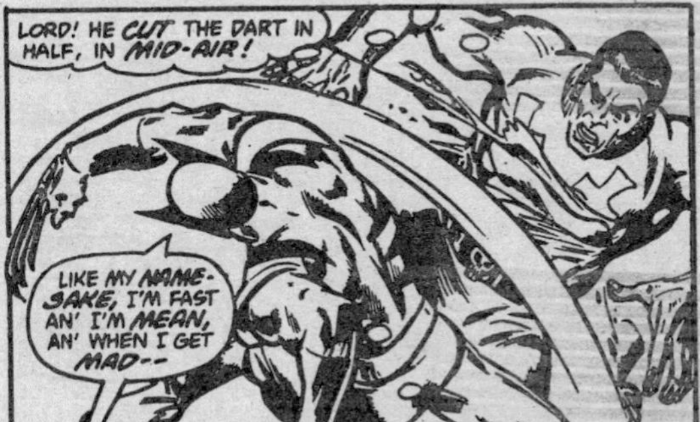
LORD! HE CUT THE DART IN HALF, IN MID-AIR!
LIKE MY NAME-SAKE, I'M FAST AN' I'M MEAN, AN' WHEN I GET MAD--
--PEOPLE GET HURT!!
HUH?!? MY CLAWS BOUNCED OFF HIS HIDE LIKE IT WAS ROCK OR STEEL!

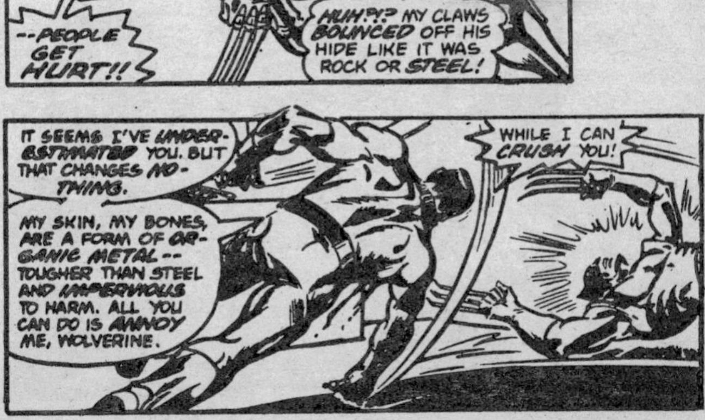
IT SEEMS I'VE UNDER-ESTIMATED YOU. BUT THAT CHANGES NO-THING.
MY SKIN, MY BONES, ARE A FORM OF OR-GANIC METAL-- TOUGHER THAN STEEL AND IMPERVIOUS TO HARM. ALL YOU CAN DO IS ANNOY ME, WOLVERINE.
WHILE I CAN CRUSH YOU!

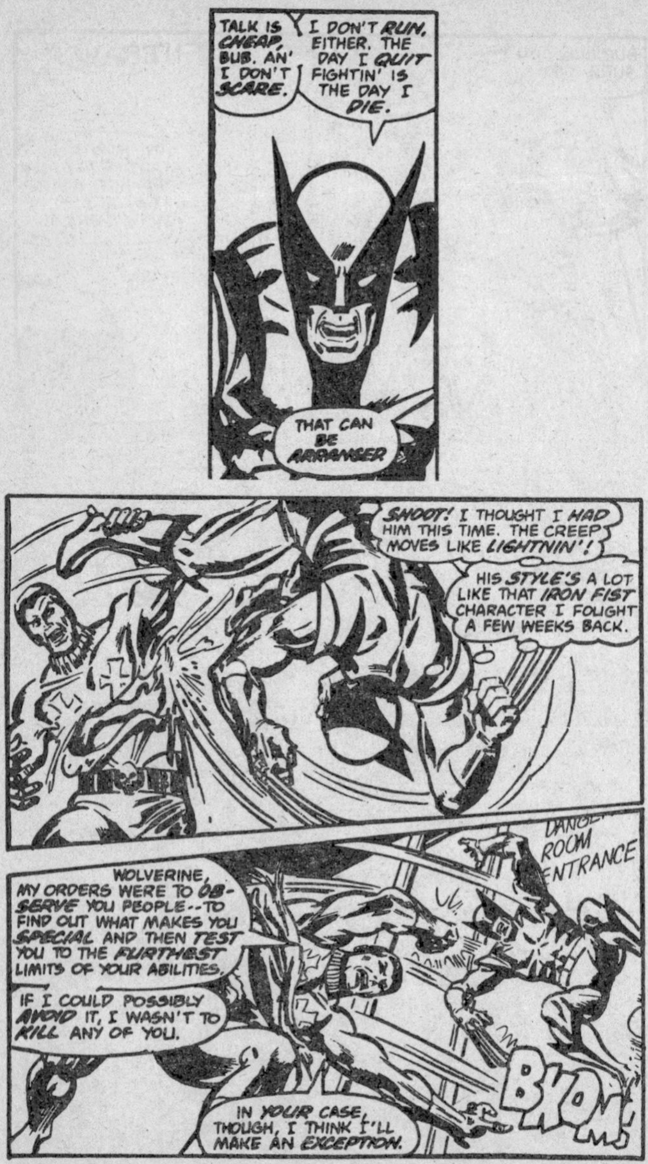

TALK IS CHEAP, BUB. AN' I DON'T SCARE.
I DON'T RUN, EITHER. THE DAY I QUIT FIGHTIN' IS THE DAY I DIE.
THAT CAN BE ARRANGED
SNOOT! I THOUGHT I HAD HIM THIS TIME. THE CREEP MOVES LIKE LIGHTNIN'!
HIS STYLE'S A LOT LIKE THAT IRON FIST CHARACTER I FOUGHT A FEW WEEKS BACK.
ROOM
ENTRANCE
WOLVERINE, MY ORDERS WERE TO OBSERVE YOU PEOPLE--TO FIND OUT WHAT MAKES YOU SPECIAL AND THEN TEST YOU TO THE FURTHEST LIMITS OF YOUR ABILITIES.
IF I COULD POSSIBLY AVOID IT, I WASN'T TO KILL ANY OF YOU.
IN YOUR CASE, THOUGH, I THINK I'LL MAKE AN EXCEPTION.
BKOOM!

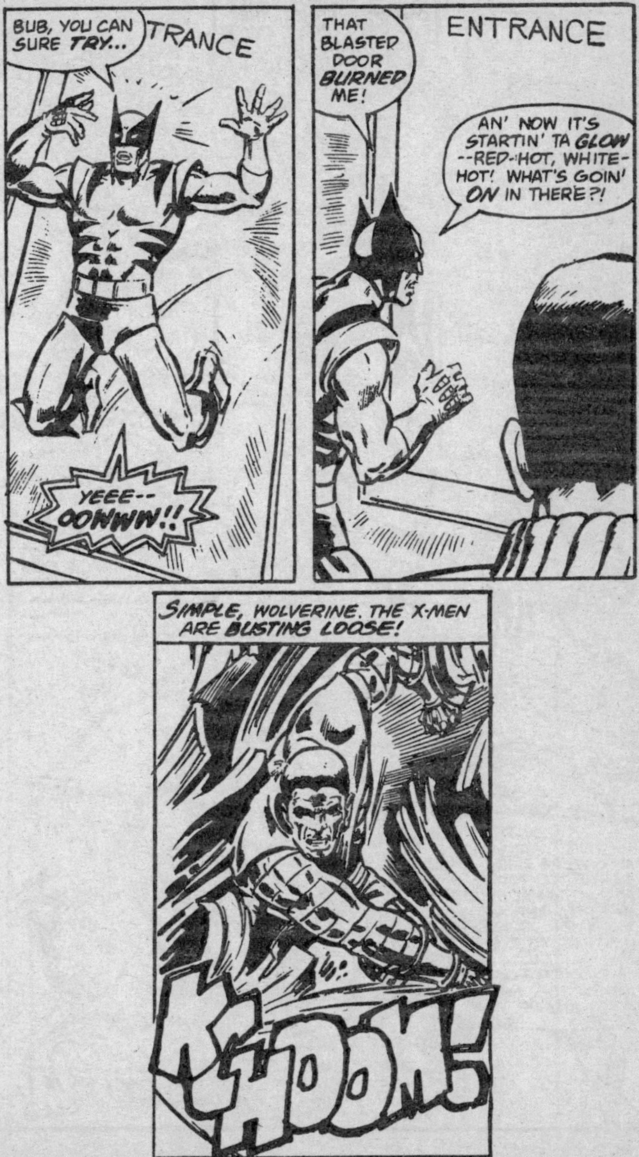

BUB, YOU CAN SURE TRY...
TRANCE
YEEE--OONWW!!
ENTRANCE
THAT BLASTED DOOR BURNED ME!
AN' NOW IT'S STARTIN' TA GLOW --RED-HOT, WHITE-HOT! WHAT'S GOIN' ON IN THERE?!
SIMPLE, WOLVERINE. THE X-MEN ARE BUSTING LOOSE!
WHOOM!

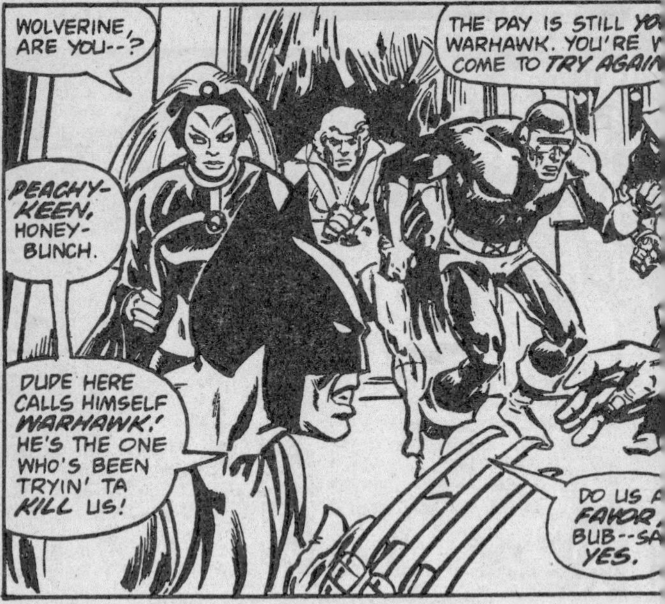
WOLVERINE, ARE YOU--?
PEACHY-KEEN, HONEY-BUNCH.
DUDE HERE CALLS HIMSELF WARHAWK! HE'S THE ONE WHO'S BEEN TRYIN' TA KILL US!
THE DAY IS STILL YO
WARHAWK. YOU'RE
COME TO TRY AGAI
DO US A
FAVOR,
BUB--SA
YES.

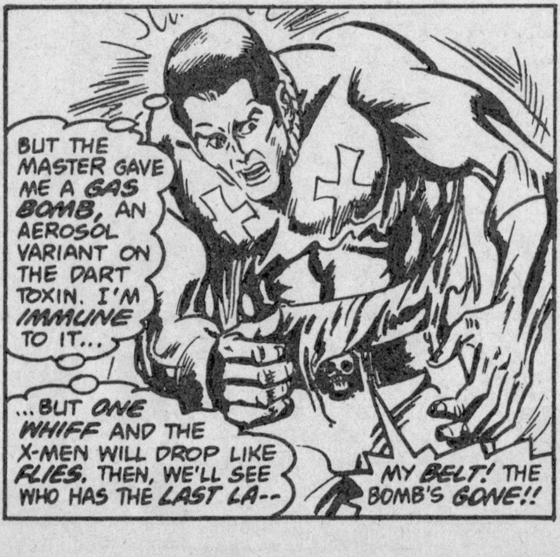
BUT THE MASTER GAVE ME A GAS BOMB, AN AEROSOL VARIANT ON THE DART TOXIN. I'M IMMUNE TO IT...
...BUT ONE WHIFF AND THE X-MEN WILL DROP LIKE FLIES. THEN, WE'LL SEE WHO HAS THE LAST LA--
MY BELT! THE BOMB'S GONE!!

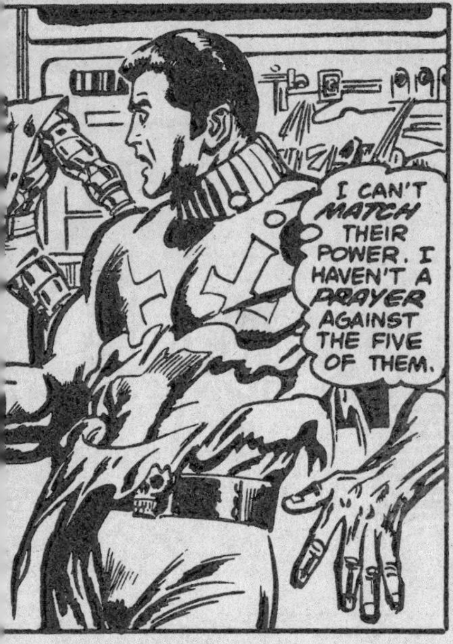
I CAN'T MATCH THEIR POWER. I HAVEN'T A PRAYER AGAINST THE FIVE OF THEM.

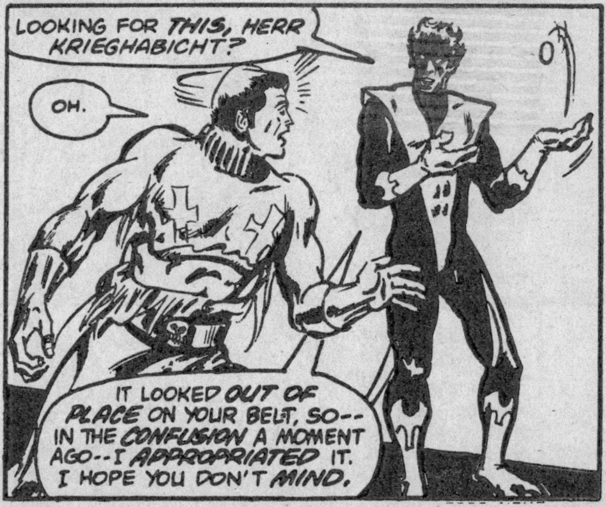
LOOKING FOR THIS, HERR KRIEGHABICHT?
OH.
IT LOOKED OUT OF PLACE ON YOUR BELT, SO-- IN THE CONFUSION A MOMENT AGO--I APPROPRIATED IT. I HOPE YOU DON'T MIND.

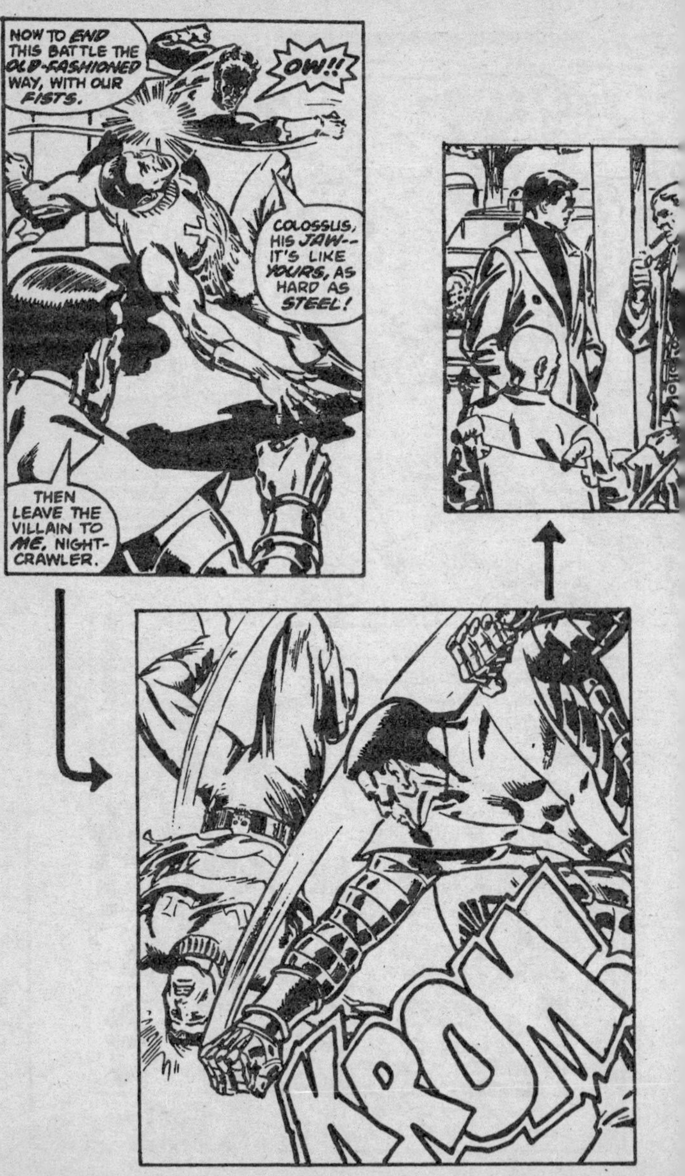
NOW TO END THIS BATTLE THE OLD-FASHIONED WAY, WITH OUR FISTS.
OW!!
COLOSSUS, HIS JAW-- IT'S LIKE YOURS, AS HARD AS STEEL!
THEN LEAVE THE VILLAIN TO ME, NIGHT-CRAWLER.
KROM

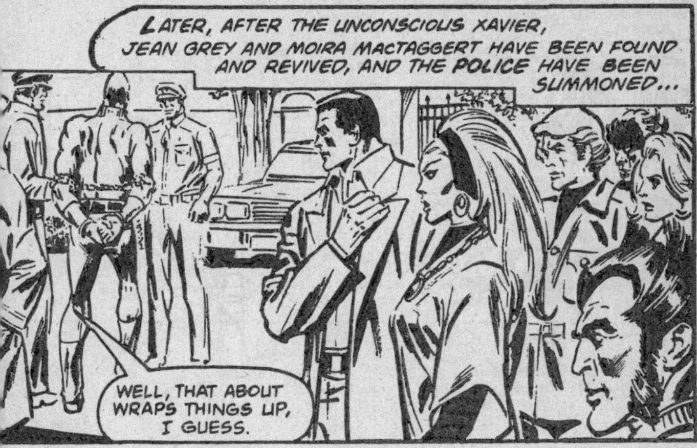
LATER, AFTER THE UNCONSCIOUS XAVIER, JEAN GREY AND MOIRA MACTAGGERT HAVE BEEN FOUND AND REVIVED, AND THE POLICE HAVE BEEN SUMMONED...
WELL, THAT ABOUT WRAPS THINGS UP, I GUESS.

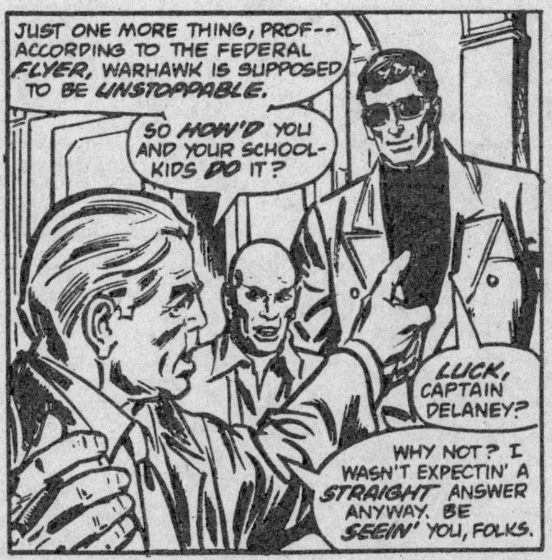
JUST ONE MORE THING, PROF-- ACCORDING TO THE FEDERAL FLYER, WARHAWK IS SUPPOSED TO BE UNSTOPPABLE.
SO HOW'D YOU AND YOUR SCHOOL-KIDS DO IT?
LUCK, CAPTAIN DELANEY?
WHY NOT? I WASN'T EXPECTIN' A STRAIGHT ANSWER ANYWAY. BE SEEIN' YOU, FOLKS.

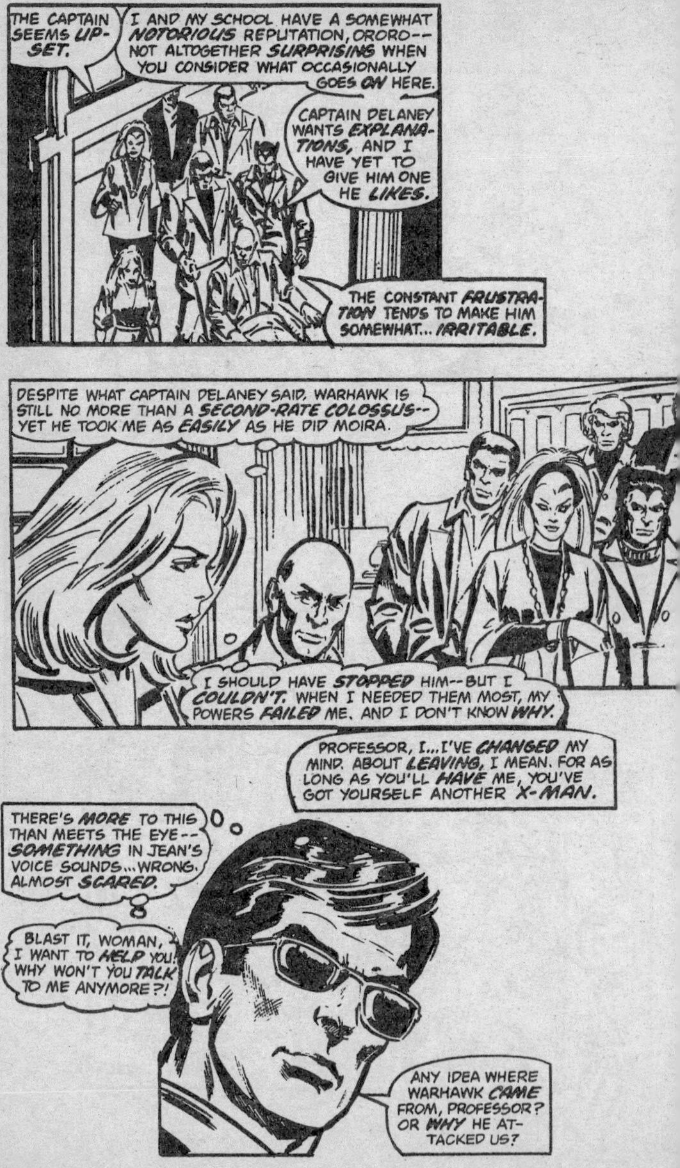
THE CAPTAIN SEEMS UP-SET.
I AND MY SCHOOL HAVE A SOMEWHAT NOTORIOUS REPUTATION, ORORO-- NOT ALTOGETHER SURPRISING WHEN YOU CONSIDER WHAT OCCASIONALLY GOES ON HERE.
CAPTAIN DELANEY WANTS EXPLANA-TIONS, AND I HAVE YET TO GIVE HIM ONE HE LIKES.
THE CONSTANT FRUSTRA-TION TENDS TO MAKE HIM SOMEWHAT... IRRITABLE.
DESPITE WHAT CAPTAIN DELANEY SAID, WARHAWK IS STILL NO MORE THAN A SECOND-RATE COLOSSUS-- YET HE TOOK ME AS EASILY AS HE DID MOIRA.
I SHOULD HAVE STOPPED HIM--BUT I COULDN'T. WHEN I NEEDED THEM MOST, MY POWERS FAILED ME. AND I DON'T KNOW WHY.
PROFESSOR, I...I'VE CHANGED MY MIND. ABOUT LEAVING, I MEAN. FOR AS LONG AS YOU'LL HAVE ME, YOU'VE GOT YOURSELF ANOTHER X-MAN.
THERE'S MORE TO THIS THAN MEETS THE EYE-- SOMETHING IN JEAN'S VOICE SOUNDS... WRONG. ALMOST SCARED.
BLAST IT, WOMAN, I WANT TO HELP YOU! WHY WON'T YOU TALK TO ME ANYMORE?!
ANY IDEA WHERE WARHAWK CAME FROM, PROFESSOR? OR WHY HE AT-TACKED US?

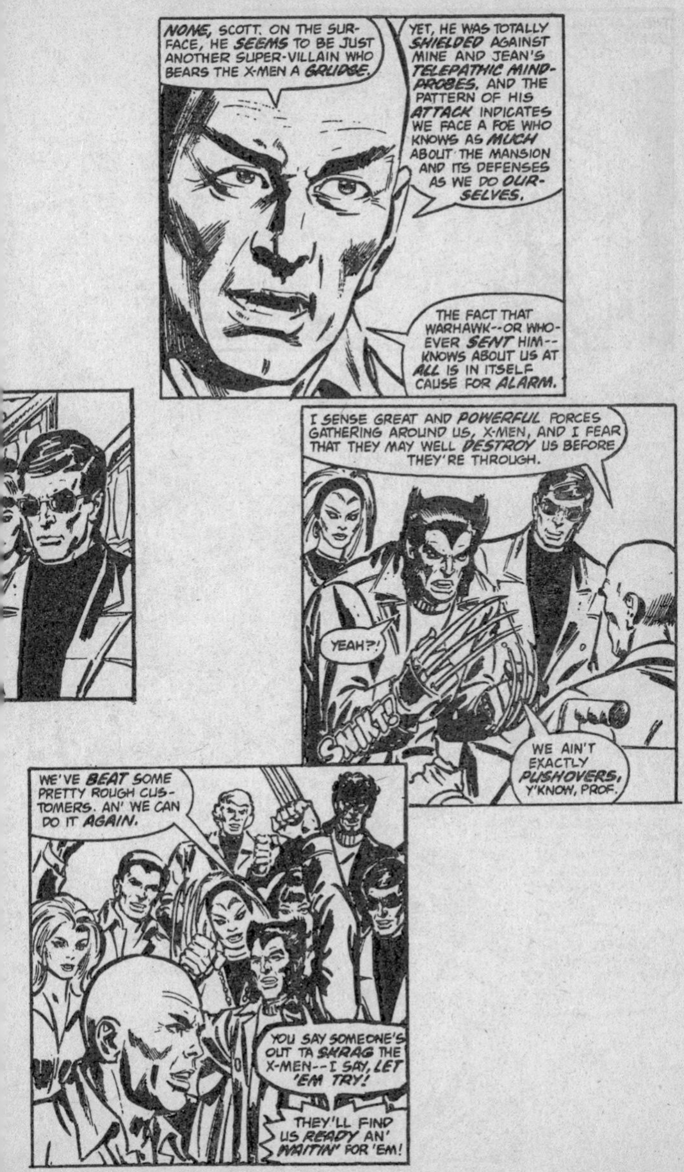
NONE, SCOTT. ON THE SURFACE, HE SEEMS TO BE JUST ANOTHER SUPER-VILLAIN WHO BEARS THE X-MEN A GRUDGE.
YET, HE WAS TOTALLY SHIELDED AGAINST MINE AND JEAN'S TELEPATHIC MIND-PROBES. AND THE PATTERN OF HIS ATTACK INDICATES WE FACE A FOE WHO KNOWS AS MUCH ABOUT THE MANSION AND ITS DEFENSES AS WE DO OURSELVES.
THE FACT THAT WARHAWK--OR WHOEVER SENT HIM--KNOWS ABOUT US AT ALL IS IN ITSELF CAUSE FOR ALARM.
I SENSE GREAT AND POWERFUL FORCES GATHERING AROUND US, X-MEN, AND I FEAR THAT THEY MAY WELL DESTROY US BEFORE THEY'RE THROUGH.
YEAH?!
SNIKT!
WE AIN'T EXACTLY PUSHOVERS, Y'KNOW, PROF.
WE'VE BEAT SOME PRETTY ROUGH CUSTOMERS. AN' WE CAN DO IT AGAIN.
YOU SAY SOMEONE'S OUT TA SHRAG THE X-MEN--I SAY, LET 'EM TRY!
THEY'LL FIND US READY AN' WAITIN' FOR 'EM!

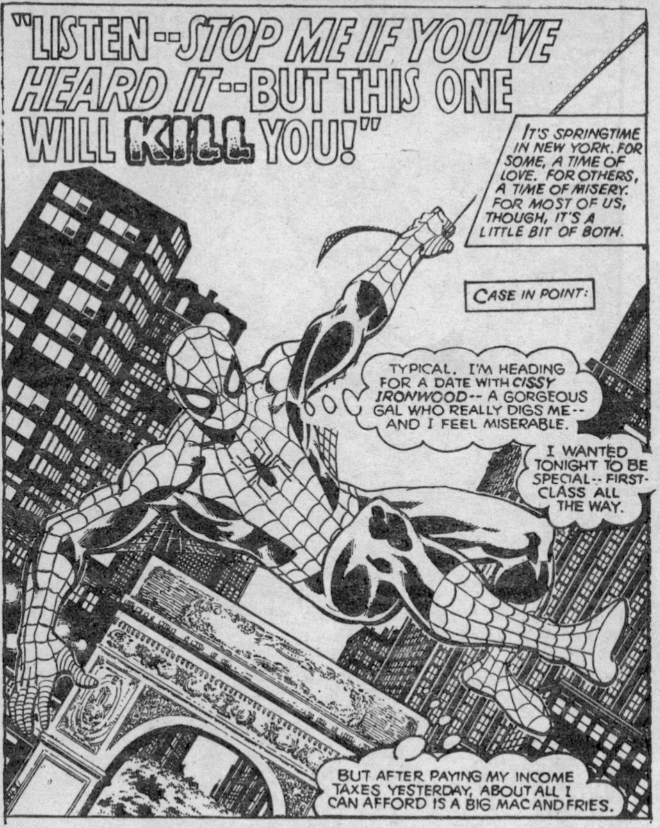
"LISTEN--STOP ME IF YOU'VE HEARD IT--BUT THIS ONE WILL KILL YOU!"
IT'S SPRINGTIME IN NEW YORK. FOR SOME, A TIME OF LOVE. FOR OTHERS, A TIME OF MISERY. FOR MOST OF US, THOUGH, IT'S A LITTLE BIT OF BOTH.
CASE IN POINT:
TYPICAL. I'M HEADING FOR A DATE WITH CISSY IRONWOOD-- A GORGEOUS GAL WHO REALLY DIGS ME-- AND I FEEL MISERABLE.
I WANTED TONIGHT TO BE SPECIAL-- FIRST-CLASS ALL THE WAY.
BUT AFTER PAYING MY INCOME TAXES YESTERDAY, ABOUT ALL I CAN AFFORD IS A BIG MAC AND FRIES.

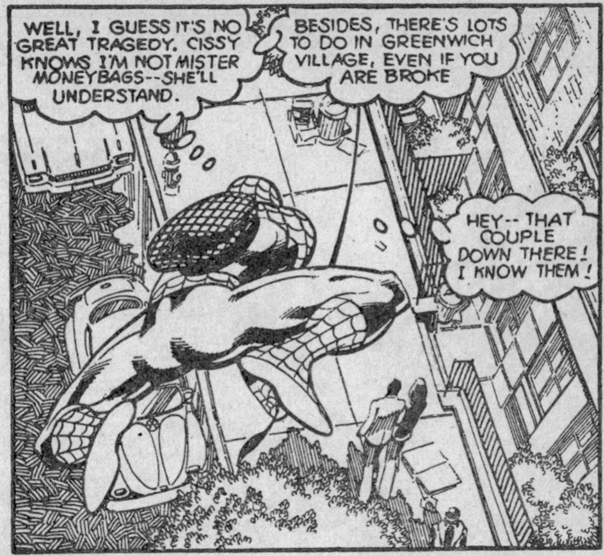
WELL, I GUESS IT'S NO GREAT TRAGEDY. CISSY KNOWS I'M NOT MISTER MONEYBAGS--SHE'LL UNDERSTAND.
BESIDES, THERE'S LOTS TO DO IN GREENWICH VILLAGE, EVEN IF YOU ARE BROKE
HEY-- THAT COUPLE DOWN THERE! I KNOW THEM!

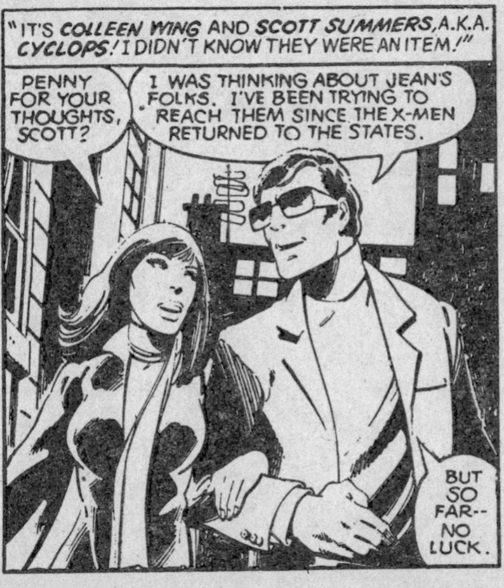
"IT'S COLLEEN WING AND SCOTT SUMMERS, A.K.A. CYCLOPS! I DIDN'T KNOW THEY WERE AN ITEM!"
PENNY FOR YOUR THOUGHTS, SCOTT?
I WAS THINKING ABOUT JEAN'S FOLKS. I'VE BEEN TRYING TO REACH THEM SINCE THE X-MEN RETURNED TO THE STATES.
BUT SO FAR-- NO LUCK.

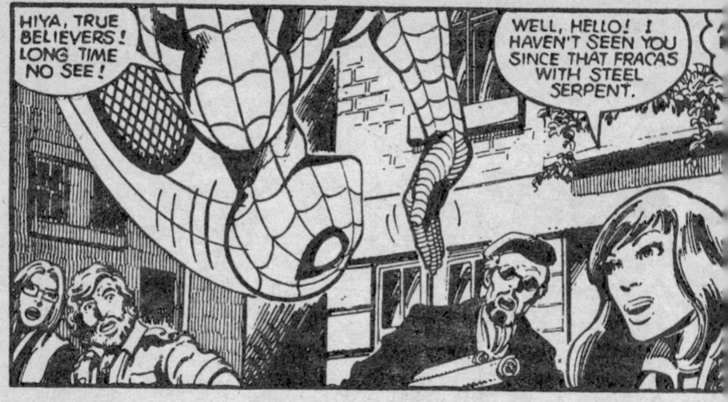
HIYA, TRUE BELIEVERS! LONG TIME NO SEE!
WELL, HELLO! I HAVEN'T SEEN YOU SINCE THAT FRACAS WITH STEEL SERPENT.

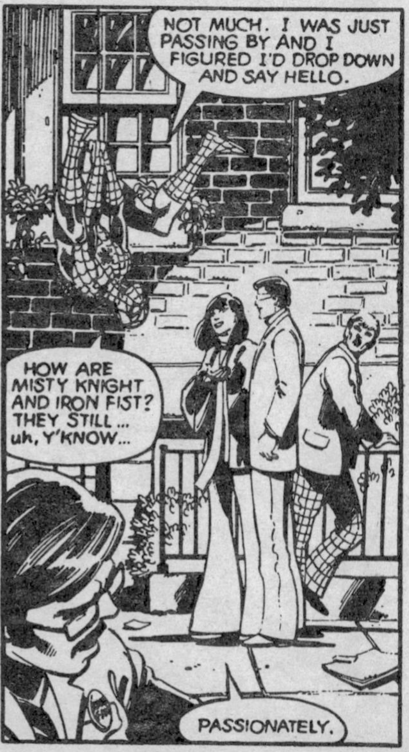
NOT MUCH. I WAS JUST PASSING BY AND I FIGURED I'D DROP DOWN AND SAY HELLO.
HOW ARE MISTY KNIGHT AND IRON FIST? THEY STILL... uh, Y'KNOW...
PASSIONATELY.

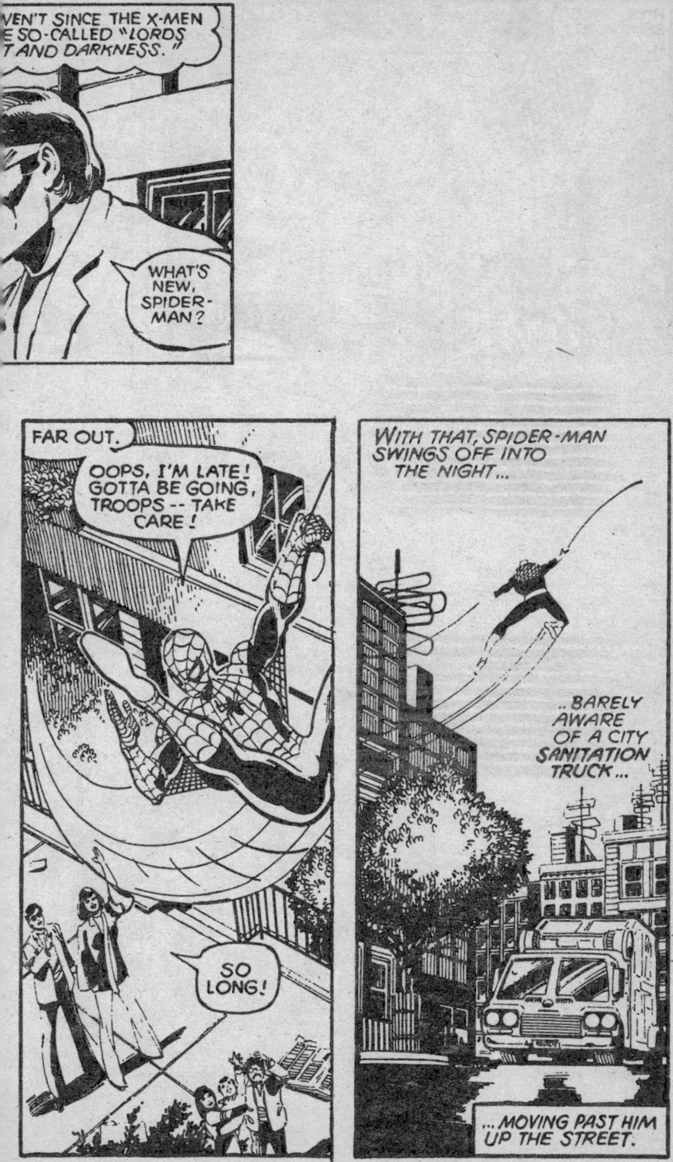
VEN'T SINCE THE X-MEN
E SO-CALLED "LORDS
T AND DARKNESS."
WHAT'S NEW, SPIDER-MAN?
FAR OUT.
OOPS, I'M LATE! GOTTA BE GOING, TROOPS -- TAKE CARE!
SO LONG!
WITH THAT, SPIDER-MAN SWINGS OFF INTO THE NIGHT...
..BARELY AWARE OF A CITY SANITATION TRUCK...
...MOVING PAST HIM UP THE STREET.

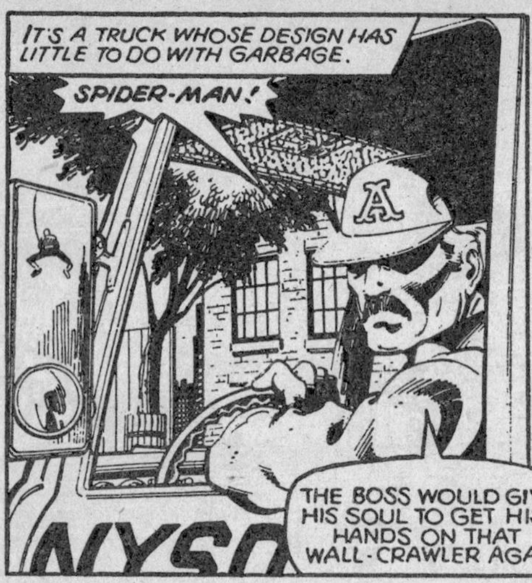
IT'S A TRUCK WHOSE DESIGN HAS LITTLE TO DO WITH GARBAGE.
SPIDER-MAN!
THE BOSS WOULD GIVE HIS SOUL TO GET HIS HANDS ON THAT WALL-CRAWLER AGAIN.
NYSD

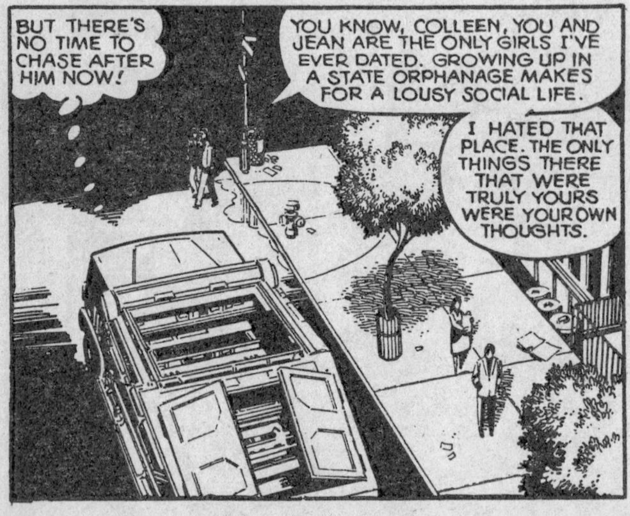
BUT THERE'S NO TIME TO CHASE AFTER HIM NOW!
YOU KNOW, COLLEEN, YOU AND JEAN ARE THE ONLY GIRLS I'VE EVER DATED. GROWING UP IN A STATE ORPHANAGE MAKES FOR A LOUSY SOCIAL LIFE.
I HATED THAT PLACE. THE ONLY THINGS THERE THAT WERE TRULY YOURS WERE YOUR OWN THOUGHTS.

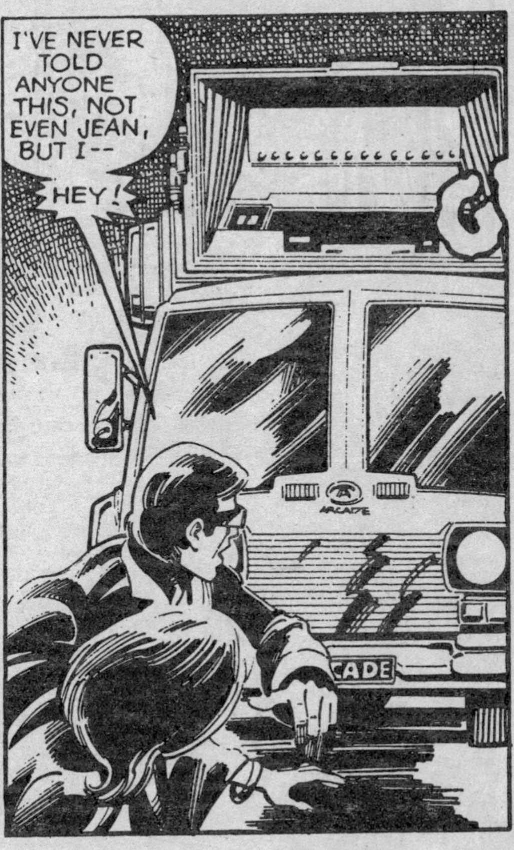
I'VE NEVER TOLD ANYONE THIS, NOT EVEN JEAN, BUT I--
HEY!
ARCADE
CADE

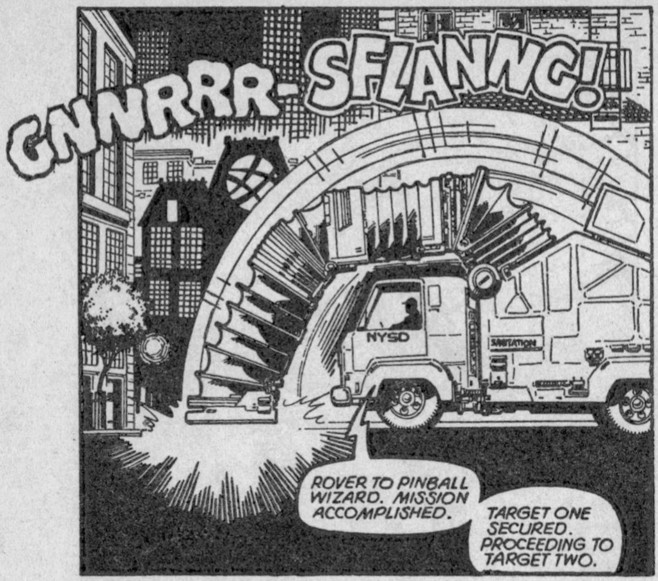
GNNRRR-SFLANNG!
NYSD
SANITATION
ROVER TO PINBALL WIZARD. MISSION ACCOMPLISHED.
TARGET ONE SECURED. PROCEEDING TO TARGET TWO.

AT THAT, MOMENT, NOT FAR AWAY...

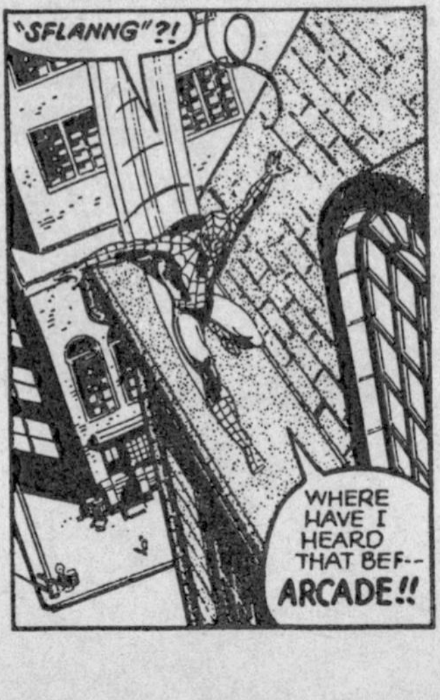
"SFLANNG"?!
WHERE HAVE I HEARD THAT BEF-- ARCADE!!

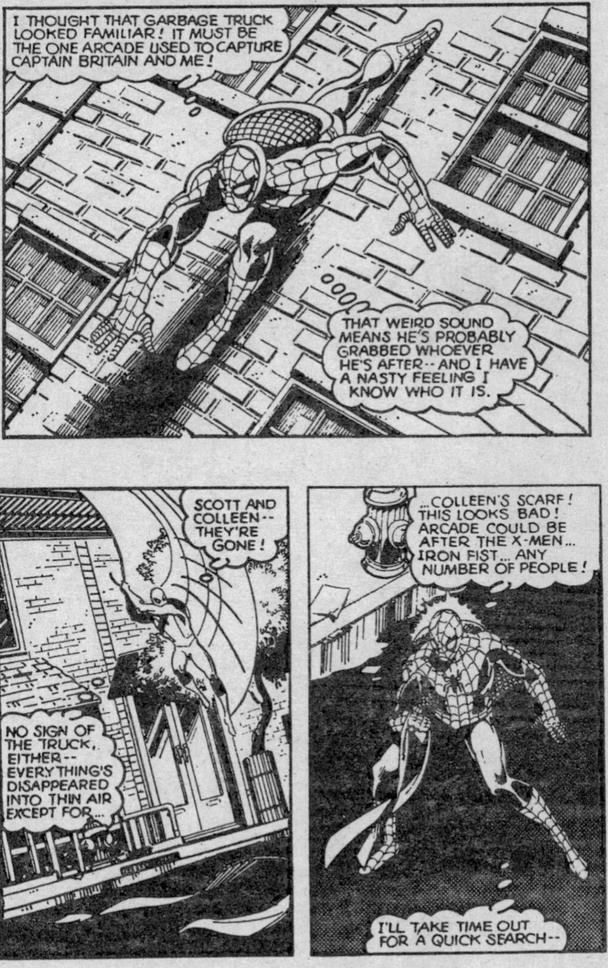

I THOUGHT THAT GARBAGE TRUCK LOOKED FAMILIAR! IT MUST BE THE ONE ARCADE USED TO CAPTURE CAPTAIN BRITAIN AND ME!
THAT WEIRD SOUND MEANS HE'S PROBABLY GRABBED WHOEVER HE'S AFTER--AND I HAVE A NASTY FEELING I KNOW WHO IT IS.
SCOTT AND COLLEEN--THEY'RE GONE!
NO SIGN OF THE TRUCK, EITHER--EVERYTHING'S DISAPPEARED INTO THIN AIR EXCEPT FOR...
...COLLEEN'S SCARF! THIS LOOKS BAD! ARCADE COULD BE AFTER THE X-MEN... IRON FIST... ANY NUMBER OF PEOPLE!
I'LL TAKE TIME OUT FOR A QUICK SEARCH--

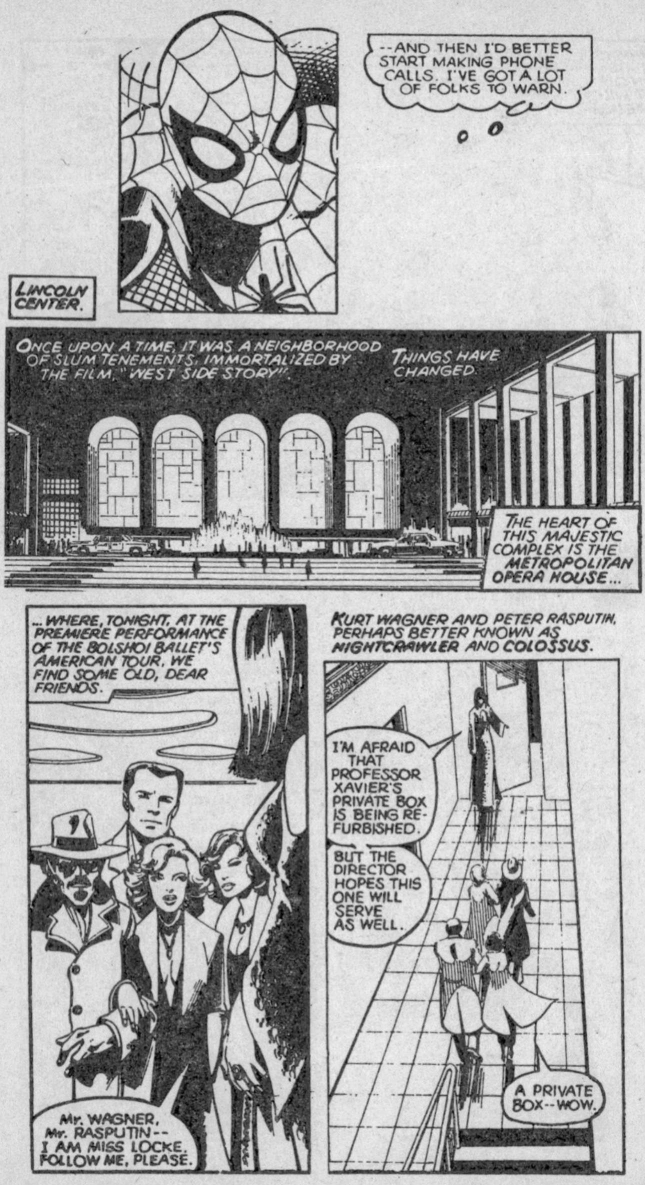
--AND THEN I'D BETTER START MAKING PHONE CALLS. I'VE GOT A LOT OF FOLKS TO WARN.
LINCOLN CENTER.
ONCE UPON A TIME, IT WAS A NEIGHBORHOOD OF SLUM TENEMENTS, IMMORTALIZED BY THE FILM, "WEST SIDE STORY".
THINGS HAVE CHANGED.
THE HEART OF THIS MAJESTIC COMPLEX IS THE METROPOLITAN OPERA HOUSE...
... WHERE, TONIGHT, AT THE PREMIERE PERFORMANCE OF THE BOLSHOI BALLET'S AMERICAN TOUR, WE FIND SOME OLD, DEAR FRIENDS.
Mr. WAGNER, Mr. RASPUTIN-- I AM MISS LOCKE. FOLLOW ME, PLEASE.
KURT WAGNER AND PETER RASPUTIN, PERHAPS BETTER KNOWN AS NIGHTCRAWLER AND COLOSSUS.
I'M AFRAID THAT PROFESSOR XAVIER'S PRIVATE BOX IS BEING RE-FURBISHED.
BUT THE DIRECTOR HOPES THIS ONE WILL SERVE AS WELL.
A PRIVATE BOX--WOW.

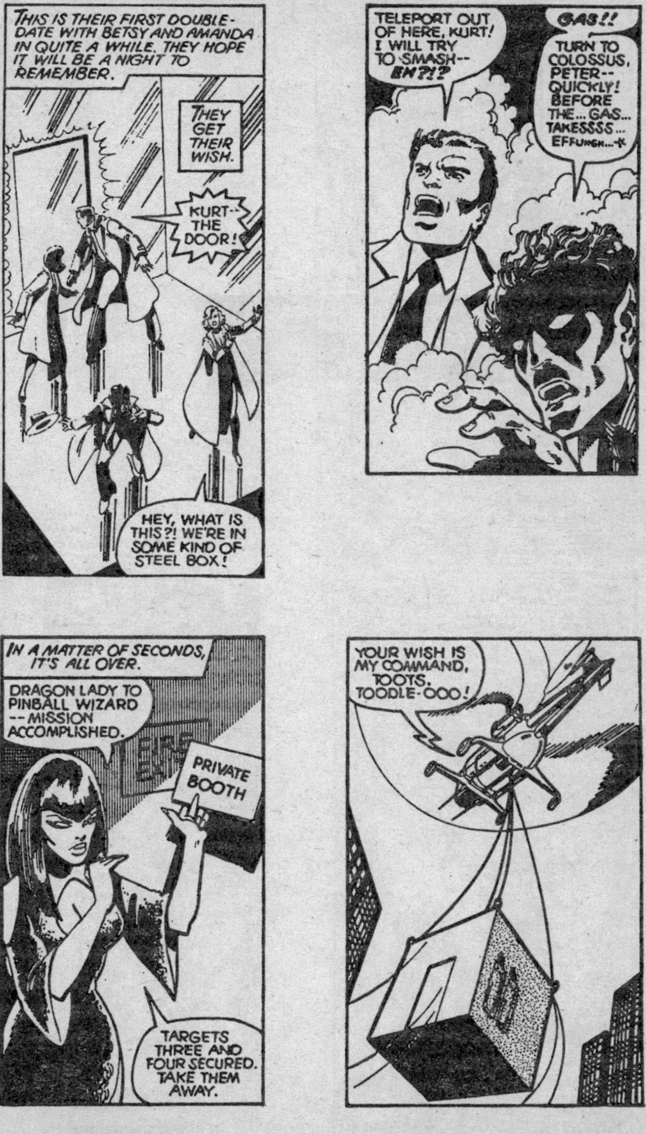
THIS IS THEIR FIRST DOUBLE-DATE WITH BETSY AND AMANDA IN QUITE A WHILE. THEY HOPE IT WILL BE A NIGHT TO REMEMBER.
THEY GET THEIR WISH.
KURT-- THE DOOR!
HEY, WHAT IS THIS?! WE'RE IN SOME KIND OF STEEL BOX!
TELEPORT OUT OF HERE, KURT! I WILL TRY TO SMASH-- EH?!?
GAS!!
TURN TO COLOSSUS, PETER-- QUICKLY! BEFORE THE... GAS... TAKESSSS... EFFUNGH...
IN A MATTER OF SECONDS, IT'S ALL OVER.
DRAGON LADY TO PINBALL WIZARD -- MISSION ACCOMPLISHED.
PRIVATE BOOTH
TARGETS THREE AND FOUR SECURED. TAKE THEM AWAY.
YOUR WISH IS MY COMMAND, TOOTS. TOODLE-OOO!

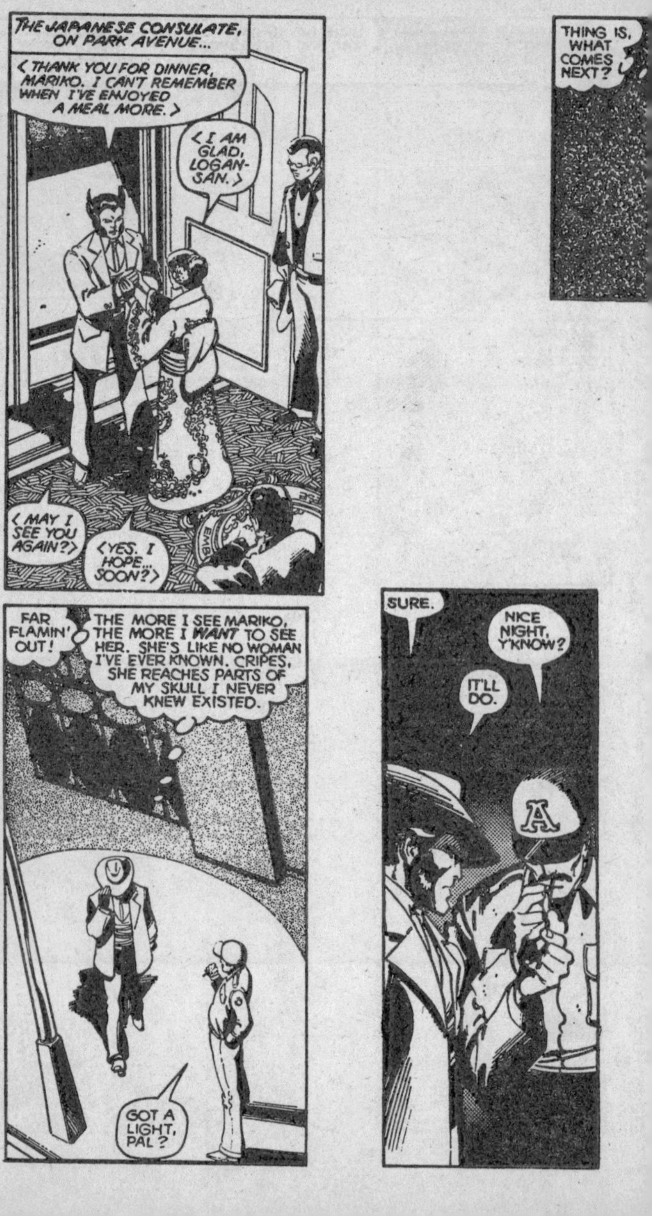
THE JAPANESE CONSULATE, ON PARK AVENUE...
<THANK YOU FOR DINNER, MARIKO. I CAN'T REMEMBER WHEN I'VE ENJOYED A MEAL MORE.>
<I AM GLAD, LOGAN-SAN.>
<MAY I SEE YOU AGAIN?>
<YES. I HOPE... SOON?>
THING IS, WHAT COMES NEXT?
FAR FLAMIN' OUT!
THE MORE I SEE MARIKO, THE MORE I WANT TO SEE HER. SHE'S LIKE NO WOMAN I'VE EVER KNOWN. CRIPES, SHE REACHES PARTS OF MY SKULL I NEVER KNEW EXISTED.
GOT A LIGHT, PAL?
SURE.
NICE NIGHT, Y'KNOW?
IT'LL DO.

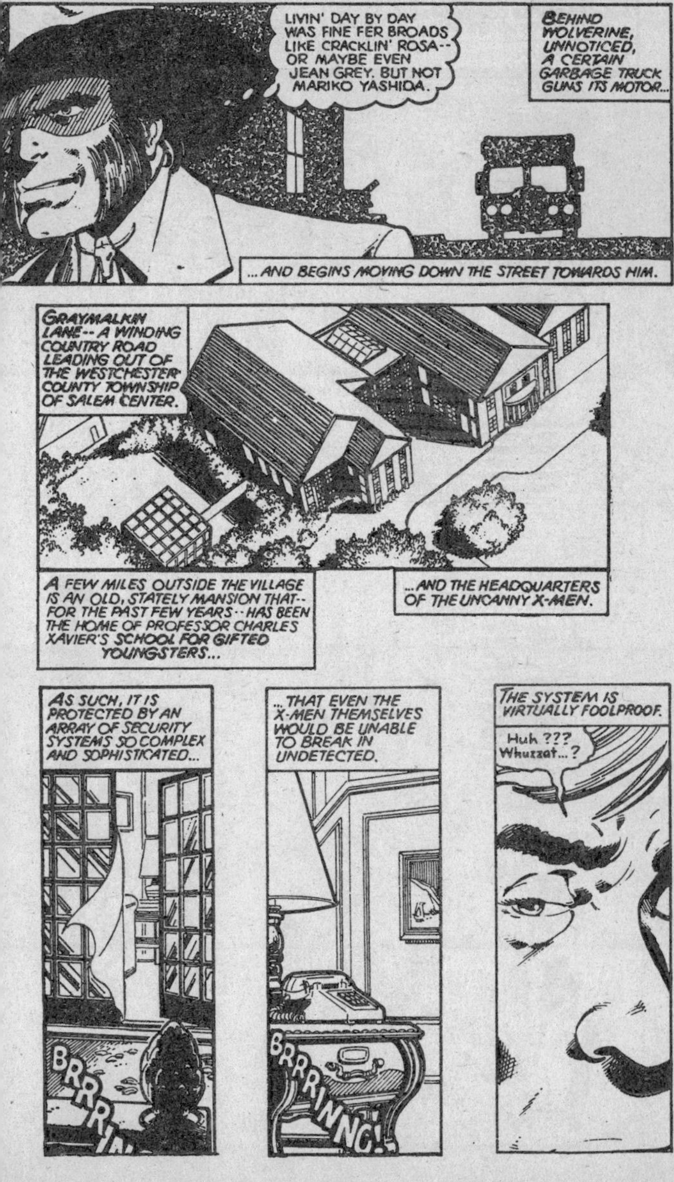
LIVIN' DAY BY DAY WAS FINE FER BROADS LIKE CRACKLIN' ROSA-- OR MAYBE EVEN JEAN GREY. BUT NOT MARIKO YASHIDA.
BEHIND WOLVERINE, UNNOTICED, A CERTAIN GARBAGE TRUCK GUNS ITS MOTOR...
...AND BEGINS MOVING DOWN THE STREET TOWARDS HIM.
GRAYMALKIN LANE-- A WINDING COUNTRY ROAD LEADING OUT OF THE WESTCHESTER COUNTY TOWNSHIP OF SALEM CENTER.
A FEW MILES OUTSIDE THE VILLAGE IS AN OLD, STATELY MANSION THAT-- FOR THE PAST FEW YEARS-- HAS BEEN THE HOME OF PROFESSOR CHARLES XAVIER'S SCHOOL FOR GIFTED YOUNGSTERS...
...AND THE HEADQUARTERS OF THE UNCANNY X-MEN.
AS SUCH, IT IS PROTECTED BY AN ARRAY OF SECURITY SYSTEMS SO COMPLEX AND SOPHISTICATED...
BRRR
...THAT EVEN THE X-MEN THEMSELVES WOULD BE UNABLE TO BREAK IN UNDETECTED.
BRRRINNG!
THE SYSTEM IS VIRTUALLY FOOLPROOF.
Huh ??? Whuzzat...?

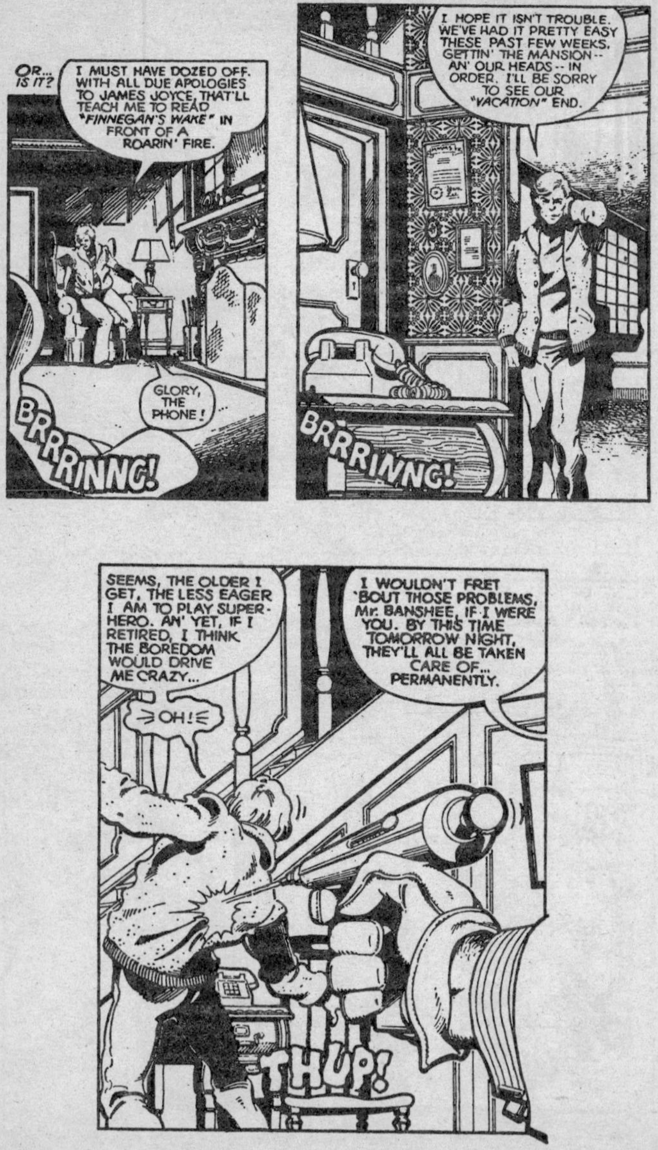
OR... IS IT?
I MUST HAVE DOZED OFF. WITH ALL DUE APOLOGIES TO JAMES JOYCE, THAT'LL TEACH ME TO READ "FINNEGAN'S WAKE" IN FRONT OF A ROARIN' FIRE.
BRRRINNG!
GLORY, THE PHONE!
I HOPE IT ISN'T TROUBLE. WE'VE HAD IT PRETTY EASY THESE PAST FEW WEEKS, GETTIN' THE MANSION-- AN' OUR HEADS -- IN ORDER. I'LL BE SORRY TO SEE OUR "VACATION" END.
BRRRINNG!
SEEMS, THE OLDER I GET, THE LESS EAGER I AM TO PLAY SUPER-HERO. AN' YET, IF I RETIRED, I THINK THE BOREDOM WOULD DRIVE ME CRAZY...
I WOULDN'T FRET 'BOUT THOSE PROBLEMS, Mr. BANSHEE, IF I WERE YOU. BY THIS TIME TOMORROW NIGHT, THEY'LL ALL BE TAKEN CARE OF... PERMANENTLY.
OH!
THUP!

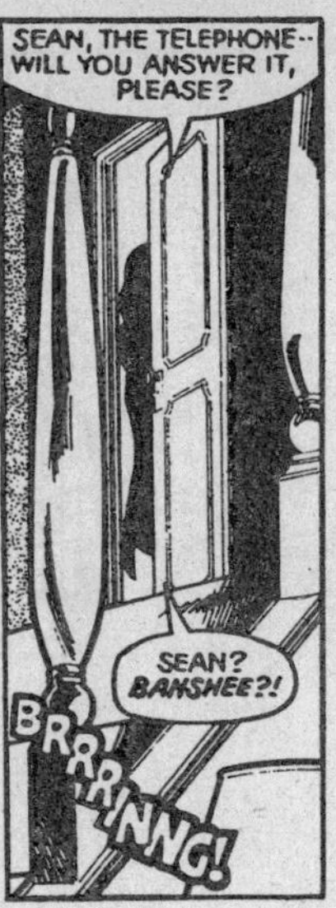
SEAN, THE TELEPHONE--
WILL YOU ANSWER IT,
PLEASE?
SEAN?
BANSHEE?!
BRRRRINNG!

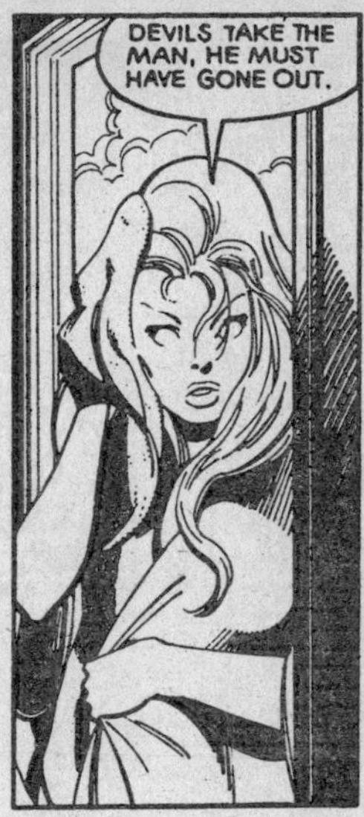
DEVILS TAKE THE
MAN, HE MUST
HAVE GONE OUT.

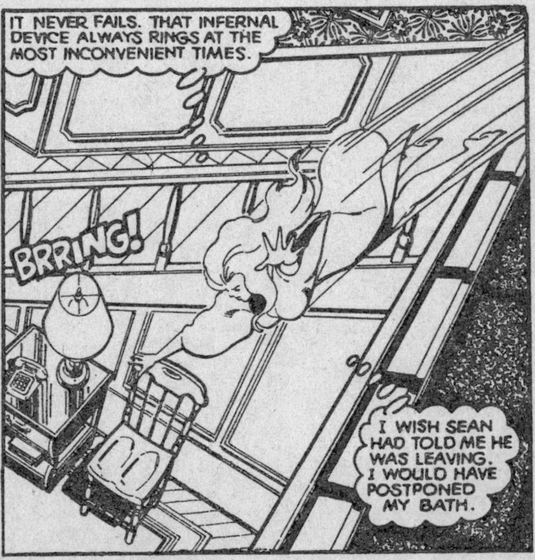
IT NEVER FAILS. THAT INFERNAL
DEVICE ALWAYS RINGS AT THE
MOST INCONVENIENT TIMES.
BRRING!
I WISH SEAN
HAD TOLD ME HE
WAS LEAVING.
I WOULD HAVE
POSTPONED
MY BATH.

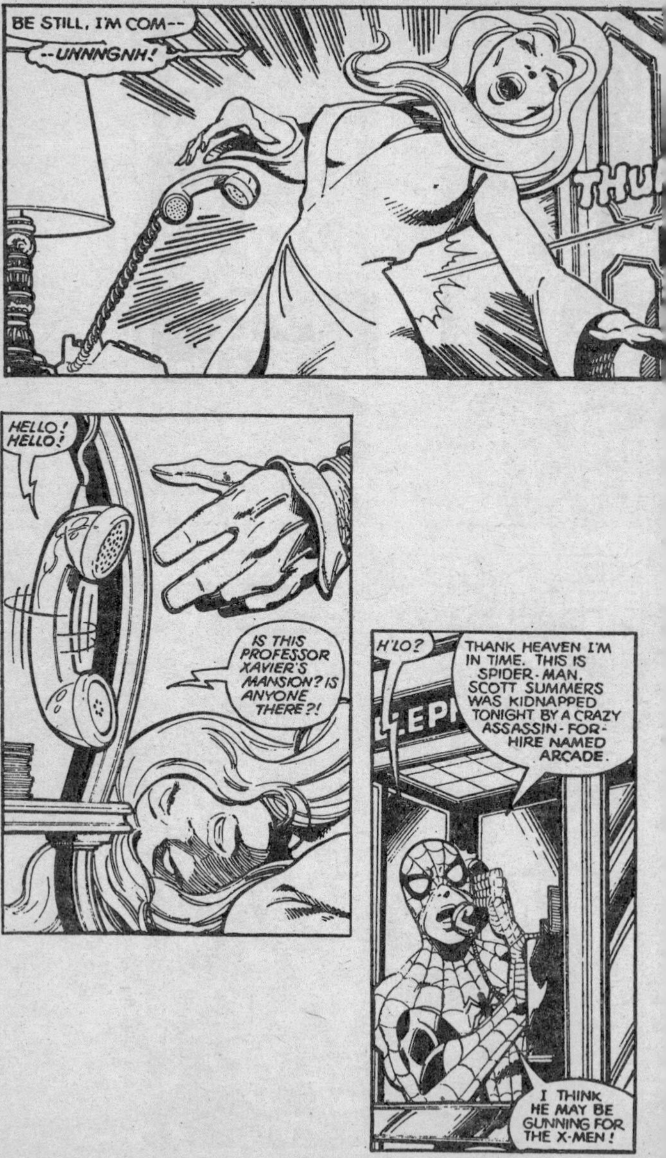
BE STILL, I'M COM--
--UNNNGNH!
HELLO! HELLO!
IS THIS PROFESSOR XAVIER'S MANSION? IS ANYONE THERE?!
H'LO?
THANK HEAVEN I'M IN TIME. THIS IS SPIDER-MAN. SCOTT SUMMERS WAS KIDNAPPED TONIGHT BY A CRAZY ASSASSIN-FOR-HIRE NAMED ARCADE.
I THINK HE MAY BE GUNNING FOR THE X-MEN!

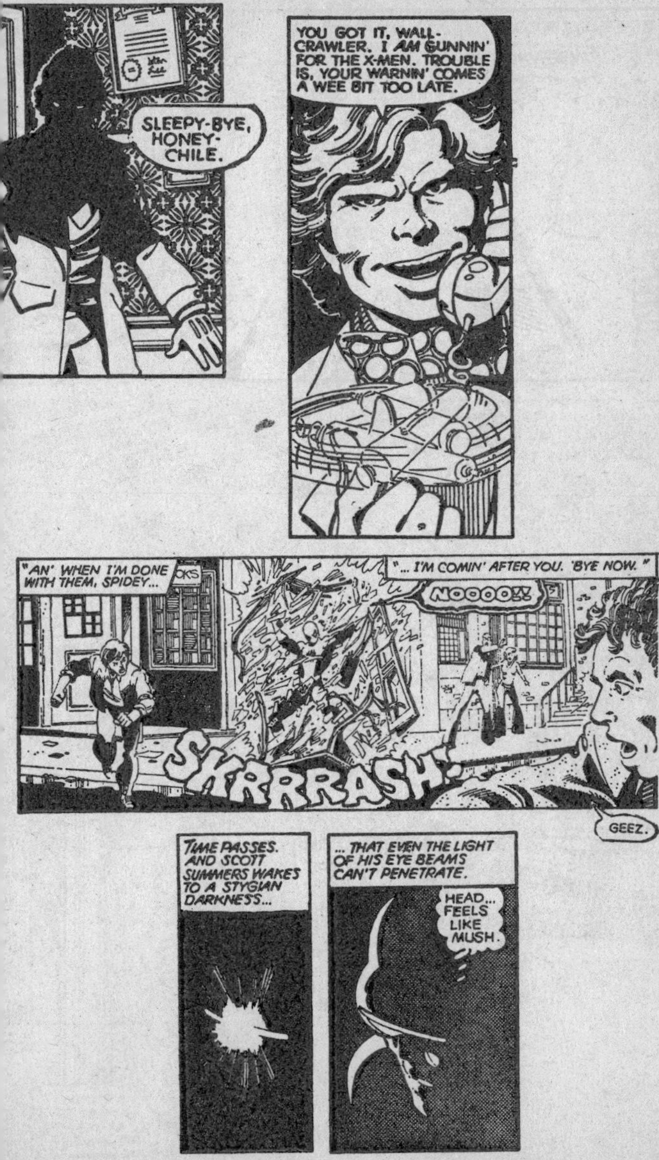
SLEEPY-BYE, HONEY-CHILE.
YOU GOT IT, WALL-CRAWLER. I AM GUNNIN' FOR THE X-MEN. TROUBLE IS, YOUR WARNIN' COMES A WEE BIT TOO LATE.
"AN' WHEN I'M DONE WITH THEM, SPIDEY...
"... I'M COMIN' AFTER YOU. 'BYE NOW."
NOOOO!!
SKRRRASH!
GEEZ.
TIME PASSES. AND SCOTT SUMMERS WAKES TO A STYGIAN DARKNESS...
... THAT EVEN THE LIGHT OF HIS EYE BEAMS CAN'T PENETRATE.
HEAD... FEELS LIKE MUSH.

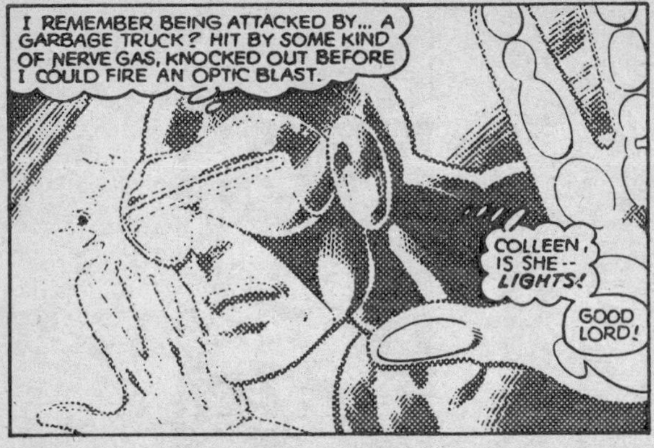
I REMEMBER BEING ATTACKED BY... A GARBAGE TRUCK? HIT BY SOME KIND OF NERVE GAS, KNOCKED OUT BEFORE I COULD FIRE AN OPTIC BLAST.
COLLEEN, IS SHE-- LIGHTS!
GOOD LORD!

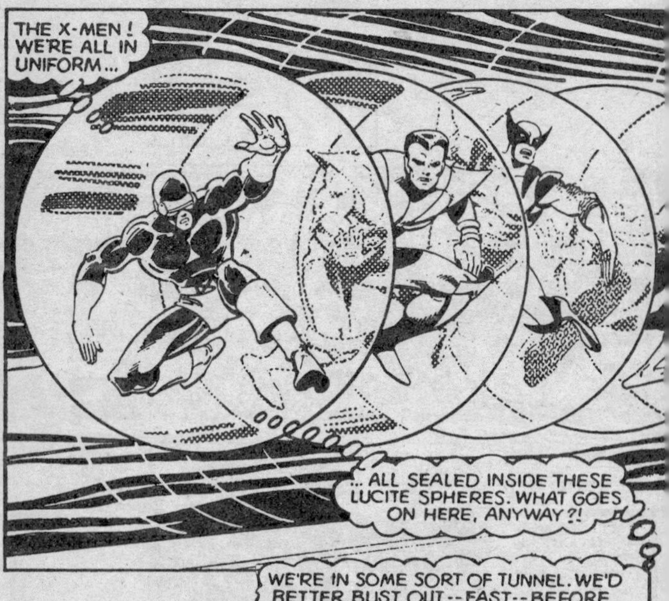
THE X-MEN! WE'RE ALL IN UNIFORM...
...ALL SEALED INSIDE THESE LUCITE SPHERES. WHAT GOES ON HERE, ANYWAY?!
WE'RE IN SOME SORT OF TUNNEL. WE'D BETTER BUST OUT--FAST--BEFORE OUR UNKNOWN HOST MAKES HIS MOVE.

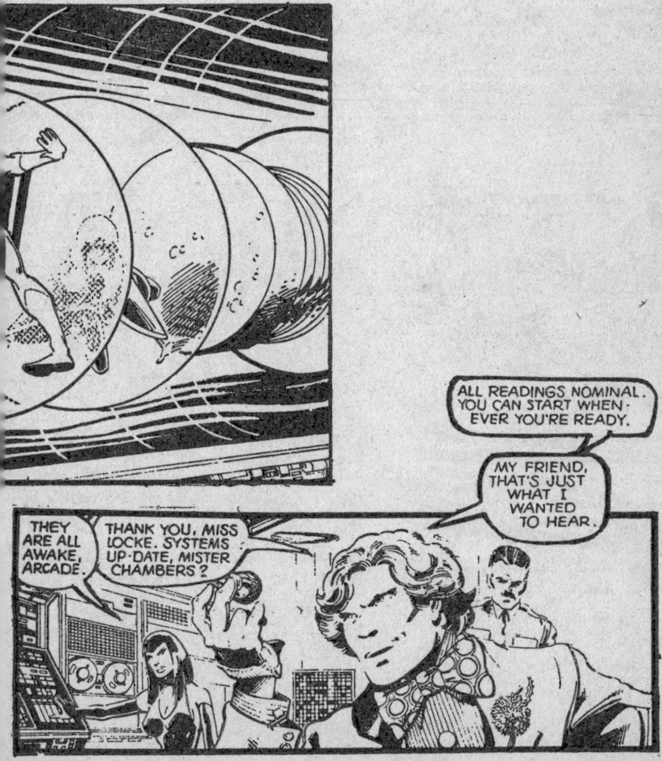
THEY ARE ALL AWAKE, ARCADE.
THANK YOU, MISS LOCKE. SYSTEMS UP-DATE, MISTER CHAMBERS?
ALL READINGS NOMINAL. YOU CAN START WHEN-EVER YOU'RE READY.
MY FRIEND, THAT'S JUST WHAT I WANTED TO HEAR.

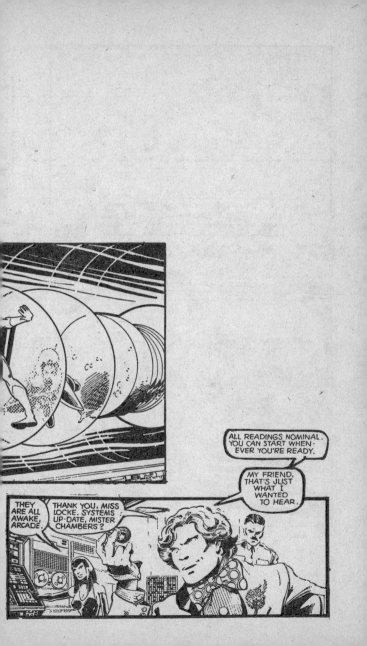

WITH GLEEFUL, PRACTICED SKILL, ARCADE DRAWS BACK THE HAMMER OF HIS MASTER PINBALL MACHINE, THAT ACTION DUPLICATED ON THE GIANT-SIZE MACHINE OUTSIDE THE CONTROL BOOTH.

LADEEZ, GENTLEMEN, AN' CHILDREN OF ALL AGES--

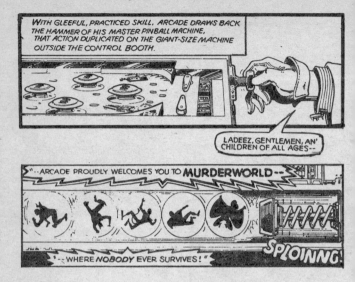

--ARCADE PROUDLY WELCOMES YOU TO **MURDERWORLD**--

"--WHERE *NOBODY* EVER SURVIVES!"

SPLOINNG!

ONE AFTER THE OTHER...

...THE BALLS SHOOT UP THE LAUNCHING TRACK--

--AND ONTO THE FACE OF THE GIANT PINBALL BOARD.

AARRRGH!

BZARK!

THE BUMPERS SEND ELECTRICAL CHARGES THROUGH THE SPHERES. AND WE'RE ROLLING SO FAST--IN SO MANY DIFFERENT DIRECTIONS AT ONCE--WE'VE NO CHANCE TO GET OUR BEARINGS.

AND THAT'S ONLY THE BEGINNING...
RAZK
BZING!

... THAT MAKES SOME OF THEM SICK, AND PREVENTS ALL OF THEM FROM BRINGING THEIR POWERS TO BEAR ON THEIR PLASTIC PRISONS...

... AS THEY ROLL HELPLESSLY TOWARDS THE MACHINE'S DEAD-BALL SLOT--EACH TO A SEPARATE, CUSTOM-DESIGNED DOOM.

THE X-MEN-- STILL GROGGY FROM THE EFFECTS OF ARCADE'S NERVE GAS-- TAKE A MERCILESS POUNDING...

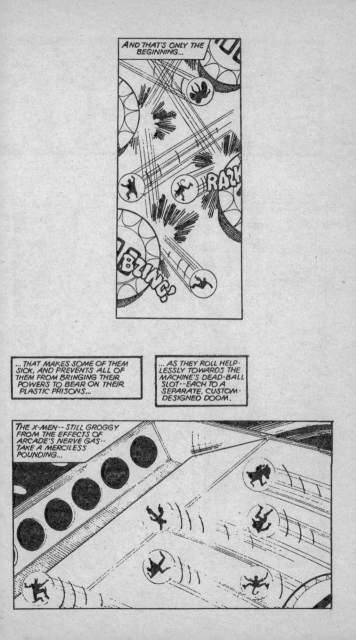

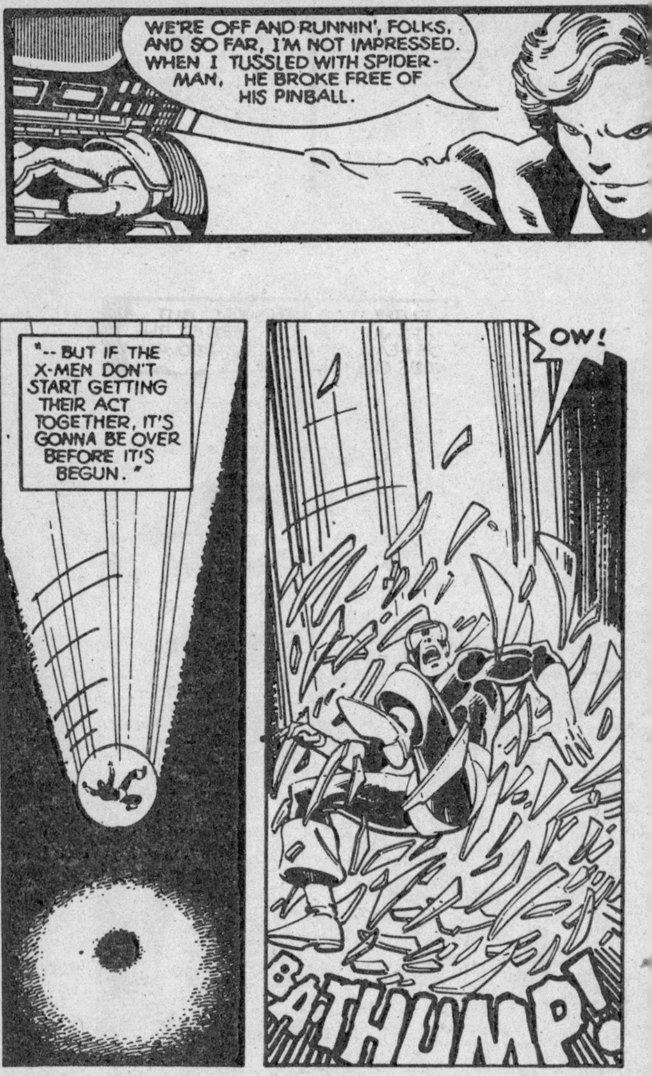
WE'RE OFF AND RUNNIN', FOLKS, AND SO FAR, I'M NOT IMPRESSED. WHEN I TUSSLED WITH SPIDER-MAN, HE BROKE FREE OF HIS PINBALL.
"-- BUT IF THE X-MEN DON'T START GETTING THEIR ACT TOGETHER, IT'S GONNA BE OVER BEFORE IT'S BEGUN."
OW!
BATHUMP!

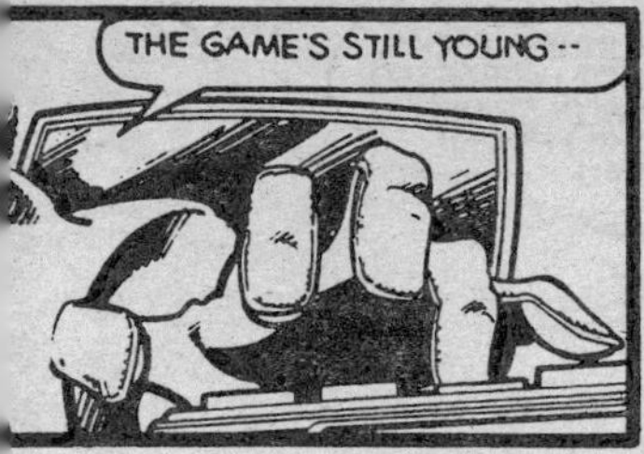
THE GAME'S STILL YOUNG --

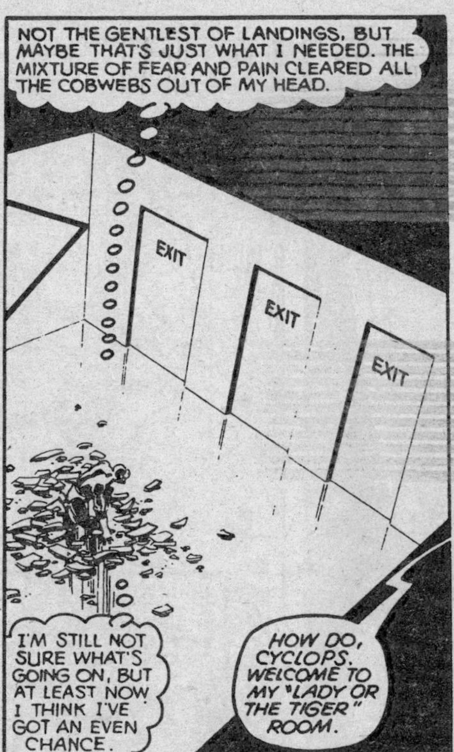
NOT THE GENTLEST OF LANDINGS, BUT MAYBE THAT'S JUST WHAT I NEEDED. THE MIXTURE OF FEAR AND PAIN CLEARED ALL THE COBWEBS OUT OF MY HEAD.
EXIT
EXIT
EXIT
I'M STILL NOT SURE WHAT'S GOING ON, BUT AT LEAST NOW I THINK I'VE GOT AN EVEN CHANCE.
HOW DO, CYCLOPS. WELCOME TO MY "LADY OR THE TIGER" ROOM.

YOU HAVE THREE DOORS-- ONE'S A WAY OUT... THE OTHER TWO LEAD TO HORRIBLE DEATHS. THE CHOICE IS YOURS.
THANKS.

RRRRR

'COURSE, WHAT HE DOESN'T REALIZE IS THAT BEHIND EACH DOOR IS A CONCRETE WALL.

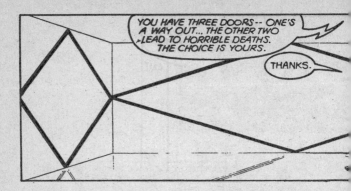

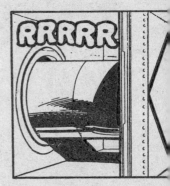

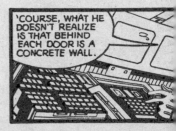

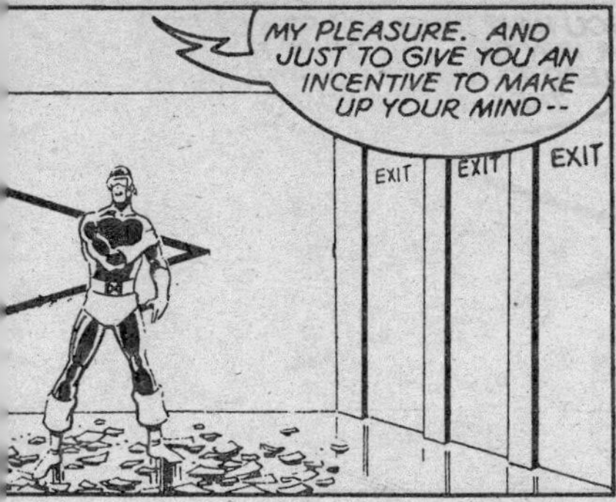
MY PLEASURE. AND JUST TO GIVE YOU AN INCENTIVE TO MAKE UP YOUR MIND--
EXIT
EXIT
EXIT

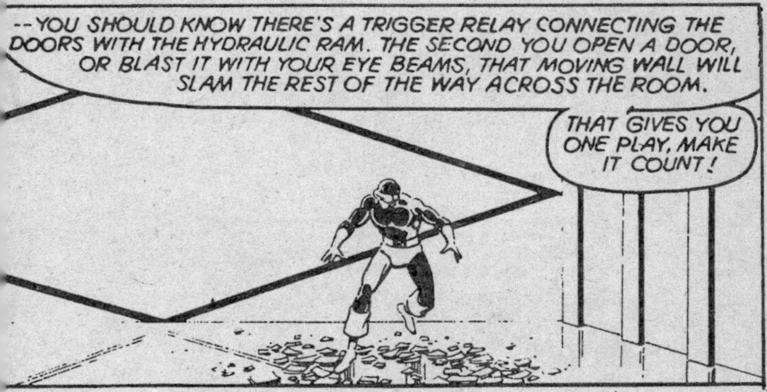
--YOU SHOULD KNOW THERE'S A TRIGGER RELAY CONNECTING THE DOORS WITH THE HYDRAULIC RAM. THE SECOND YOU OPEN A DOOR, OR BLAST IT WITH YOUR EYE BEAMS, THAT MOVING WALL WILL SLAM THE REST OF THE WAY ACROSS THE ROOM.
THAT GIVES YOU ONE PLAY, MAKE IT COUNT!

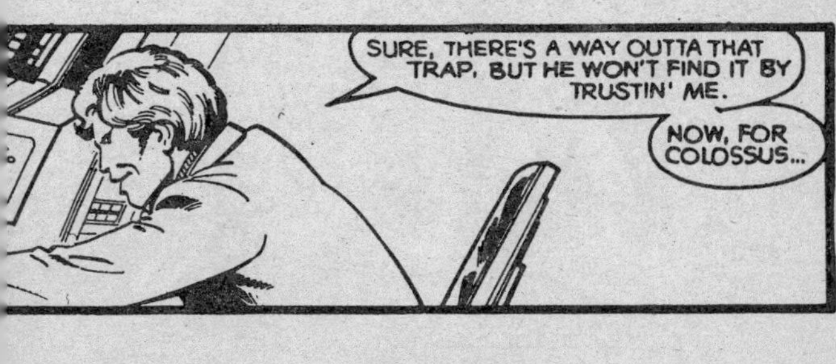
SURE, THERE'S A WAY OUTTA THAT TRAP. BUT HE WON'T FIND IT BY TRUSTIN' ME.
NOW, FOR COLOSSUS...

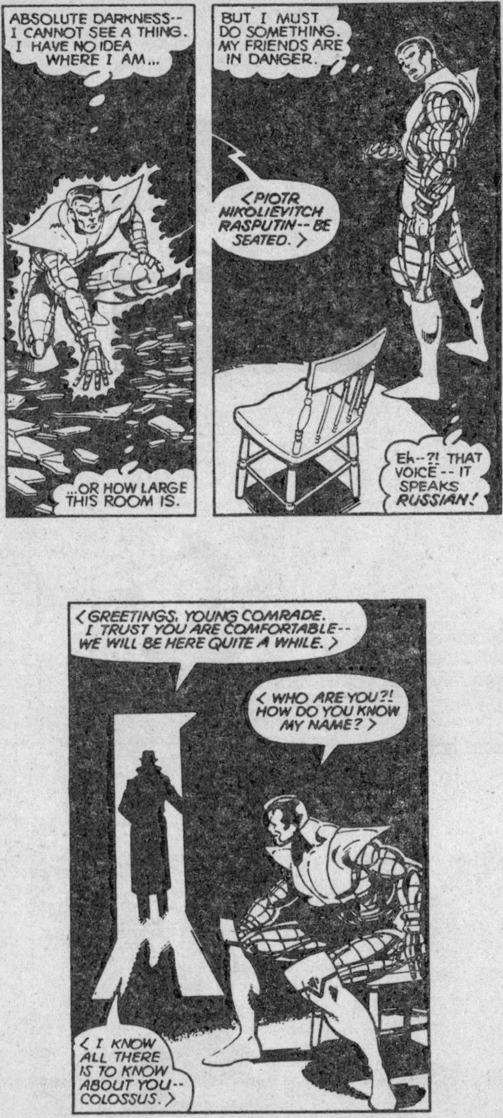
ABSOLUTE DARKNESS-- I CANNOT SEE A THING. I HAVE NO IDEA WHERE I AM...
...OR HOW LARGE THIS ROOM IS.
BUT I MUST DO SOMETHING. MY FRIENDS ARE IN DANGER.
<PIOTR NIKOLIEVITCH RASPUTIN-- BE SEATED.>
Eh--?! THAT VOICE -- IT SPEAKS RUSSIAN!
<GREETINGS, YOUNG COMRADE. I TRUST YOU ARE COMFORTABLE-- WE WILL BE HERE QUITE A WHILE.>
<WHO ARE YOU?! HOW DO YOU KNOW MY NAME?>
<I KNOW ALL THERE IS TO KNOW ABOUT YOU-- COLOSSUS.>

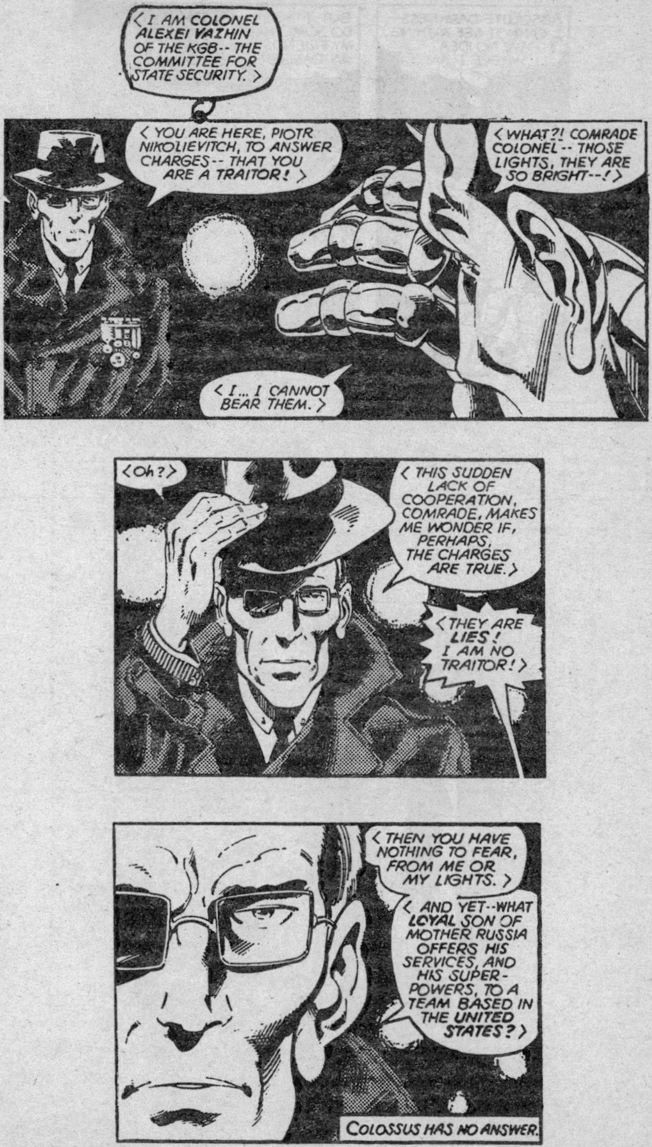
< I AM COLONEL ALEXEI VAZHIN OF THE KGB-- THE COMMITTEE FOR STATE SECURITY. >
< YOU ARE HERE, PIOTR NIKOLIEVITCH, TO ANSWER CHARGES-- THAT YOU ARE A TRAITOR! >
< WHAT?! COMRADE COLONEL -- THOSE LIGHTS, THEY ARE SO BRIGHT--! >
< I... I CANNOT BEAR THEM. >
<Oh?>
< THIS SUDDEN LACK OF COOPERATION, COMRADE, MAKES ME WONDER IF, PERHAPS, THE CHARGES ARE TRUE. >
< THEY ARE LIES! I AM NO TRAITOR! >
< THEN YOU HAVE NOTHING TO FEAR, FROM ME OR MY LIGHTS. >
< AND YET--WHAT LOYAL SON OF MOTHER RUSSIA OFFERS HIS SERVICES, AND HIS SUPER-POWERS, TO A TEAM BASED IN THE UNITED STATES? >
COLOSSUS HAS NO ANSWER.

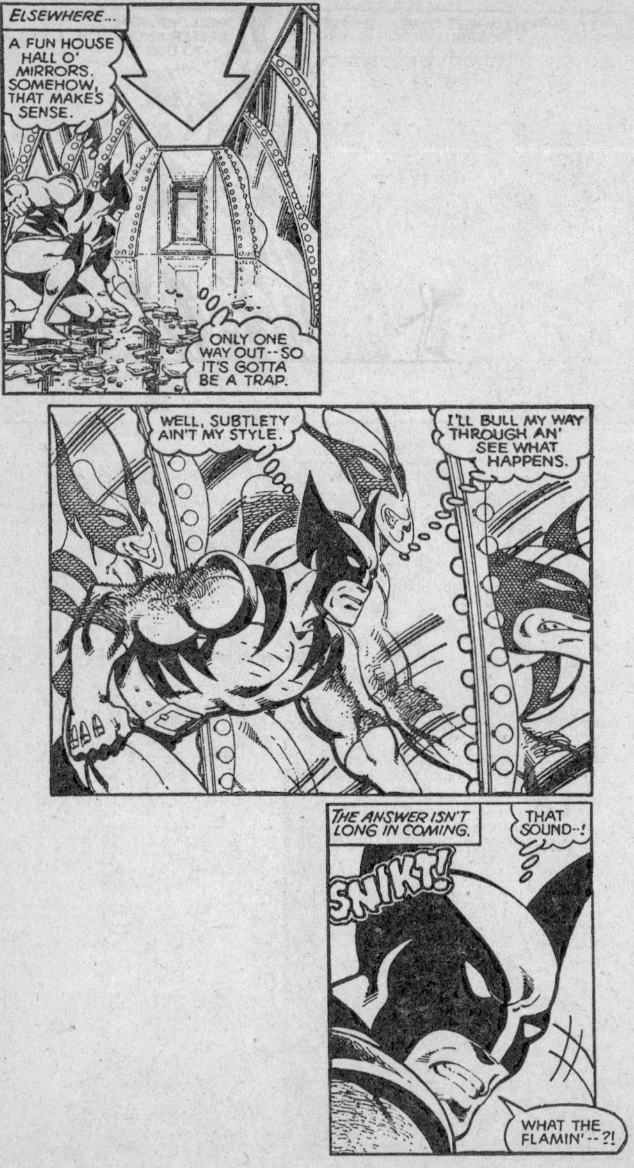
ELSEWHERE...
A FUN HOUSE HALL O' MIRRORS. SOMEHOW, THAT MAKES SENSE.
ONLY ONE WAY OUT--SO IT'S GOTTA BE A TRAP.
WELL, SUBTLETY AIN'T MY STYLE.
I'LL BULL MY WAY THROUGH AN' SEE WHAT HAPPENS.
THE ANSWER ISN'T LONG IN COMING.
THAT SOUND--!
SNIKT!
WHAT THE FLAMIN'--?!

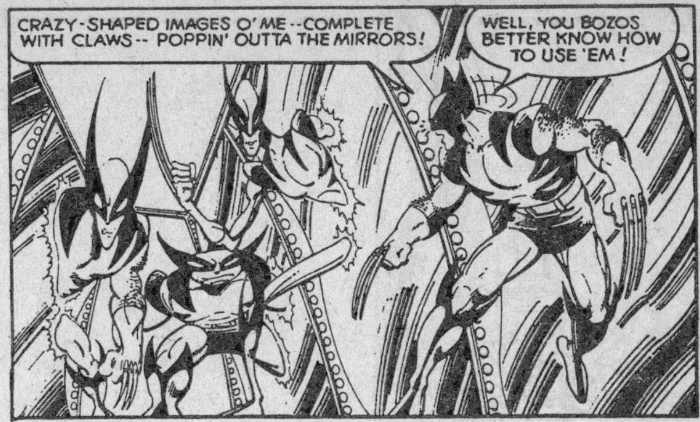
CRAZY-SHAPED IMAGES O' ME--COMPLETE WITH CLAWS-- POPPIN' OUTTA THE MIRRORS!
WELL, YOU BOZOS BETTER KNOW HOW TO USE 'EM!

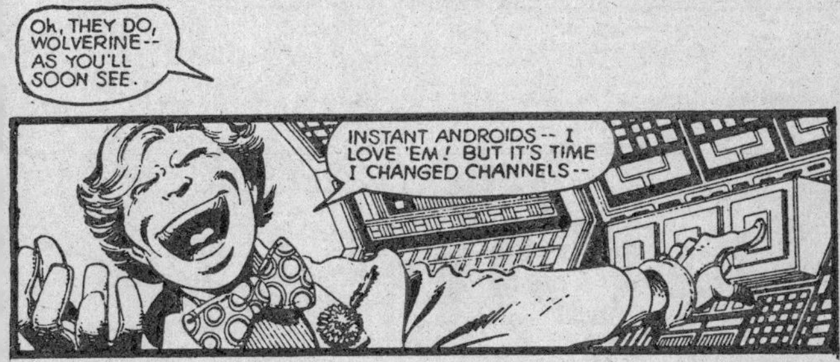
Oh, THEY DO, WOLVERINE-- AS YOU'LL SOON SEE.
INSTANT ANDROIDS-- I LOVE 'EM! BUT IT'S TIME I CHANGED CHANNELS--

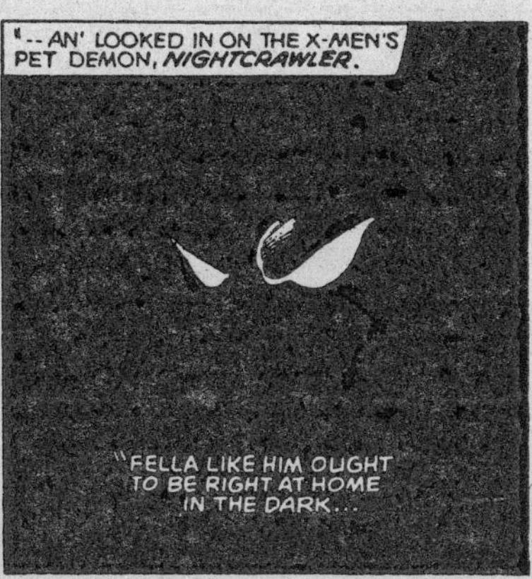
"--AN' LOOKED IN ON THE X-MEN'S PET DEMON, NIGHTCRAWLER.
"FELLA LIKE HIM OUGHT TO BE RIGHT AT HOME IN THE DARK...

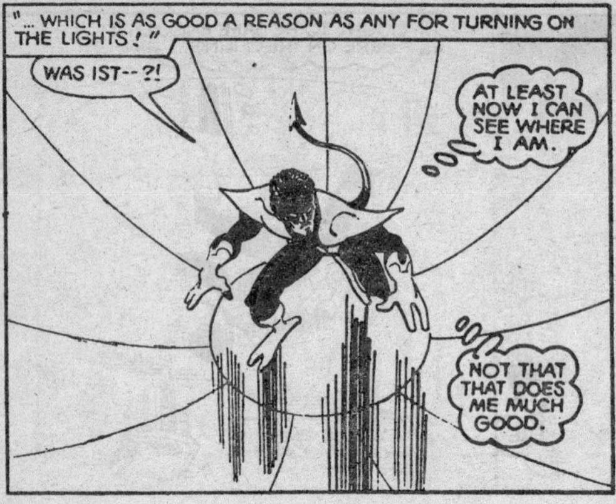
"... WHICH IS AS GOOD A REASON AS ANY FOR TURNING ON THE LIGHTS!"
WAS IST--?!
AT LEAST NOW I CAN SEE WHERE I AM.
NOT THAT THAT DOES ME MUCH GOOD.

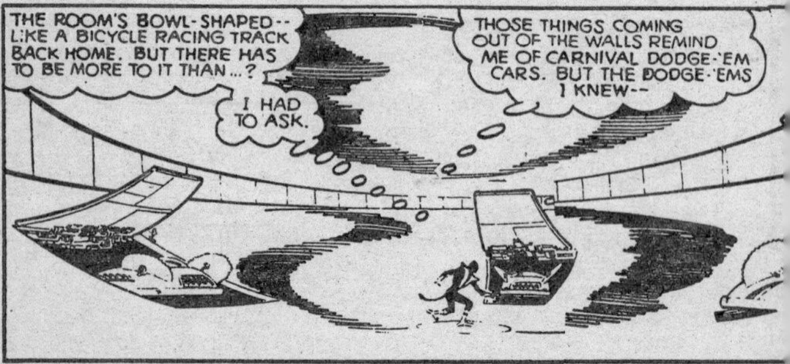
THE ROOM'S BOWL-SHAPED--LIKE A BICYCLE RACING TRACK BACK HOME. BUT THERE HAS TO BE MORE TO IT THAN...?
I HAD TO ASK.
THOSE THINGS COMING OUT OF THE WALLS REMIND ME OF CARNIVAL DODGE-'EM CARS. BUT THE DODGE-'EMS I KNEW--

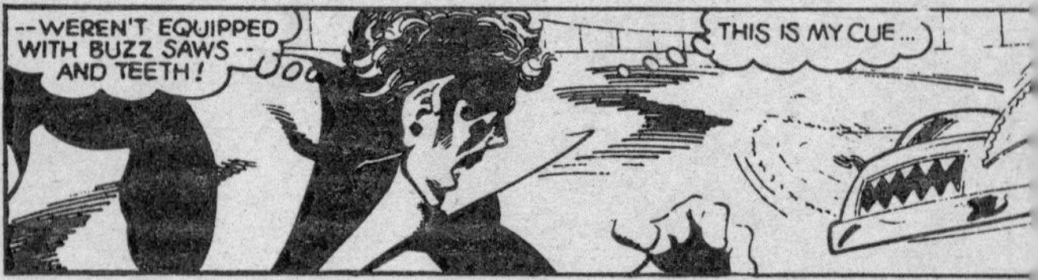
--WEREN'T EQUIPPED WITH BUZZ SAWS--AND TEETH!
THIS IS MY CUE...

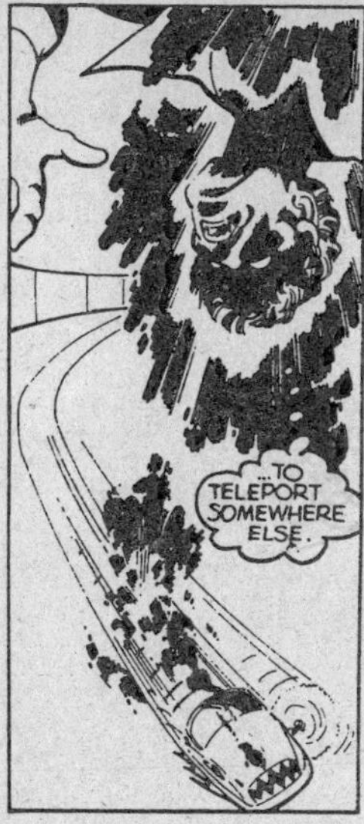
...TO TELEPORT SOMEWHERE ELSE.

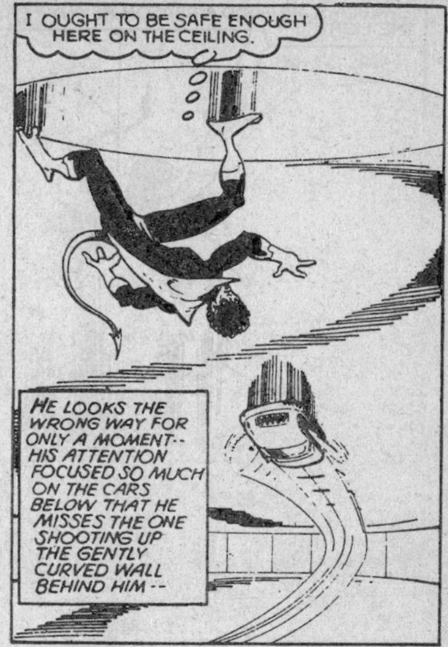
I OUGHT TO BE SAFE ENOUGH HERE ON THE CEILING.
HE LOOKS THE WRONG WAY FOR ONLY A MOMENT-- HIS ATTENTION FOCUSED SO MUCH ON THE CARS BELOW THAT HE MISSES THE ONE SHOOTING UP THE GENTLY CURVED WALL BEHIND HIM--

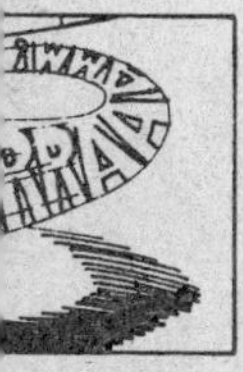

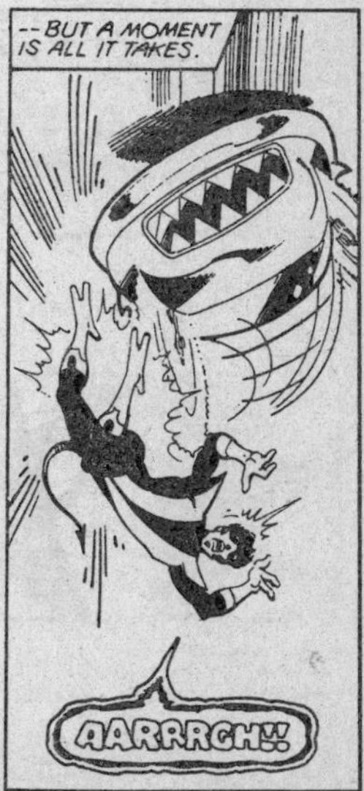
--BUT A MOMENT IS ALL IT TAKES.
AARRRGH!!

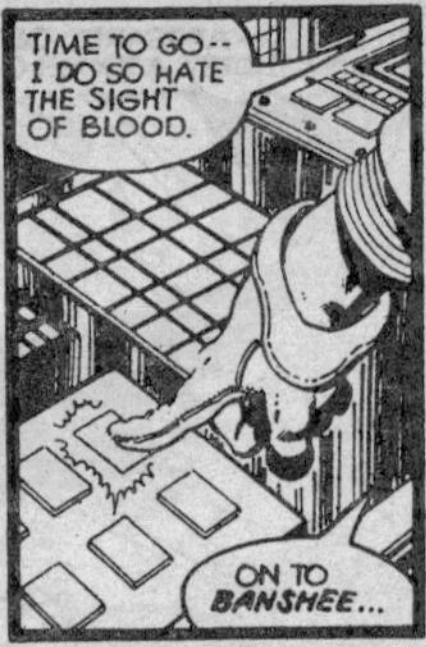
TIME TO GO-- I DO SO HATE THE SIGHT OF BLOOD.
ON TO BANSHEE...

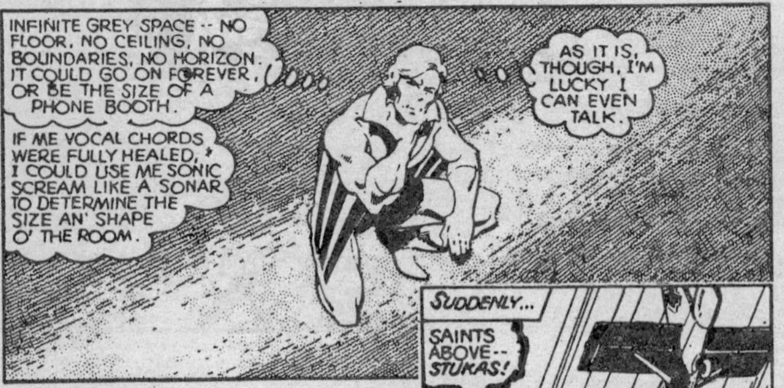
INFINITE GREY SPACE -- NO FLOOR, NO CEILING, NO BOUNDARIES, NO HORIZON. IT COULD GO ON FOREVER, OR BE THE SIZE OF A PHONE BOOTH.
IF ME VOCAL CHORDS WERE FULLY HEALED, I COULD USE ME SONIC SCREAM LIKE A SONAR TO DETERMINE THE SIZE AN' SHAPE O' THE ROOM.
AS IT IS, THOUGH, I'M LUCKY I CAN EVEN TALK.

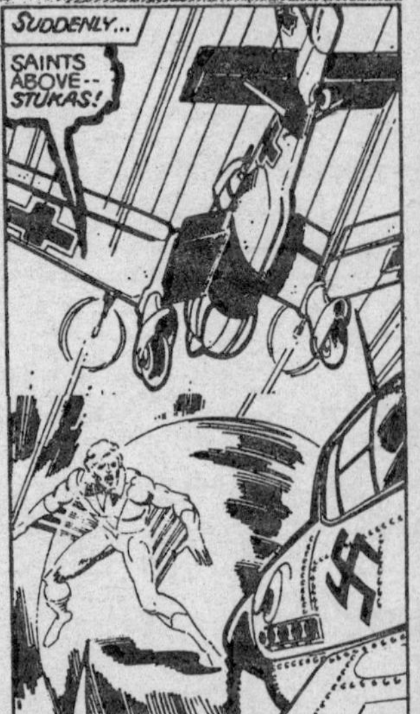
SUDDENLY...
SAINTS ABOVE-- STUKAS!
I'M BEIN' STRAFED!

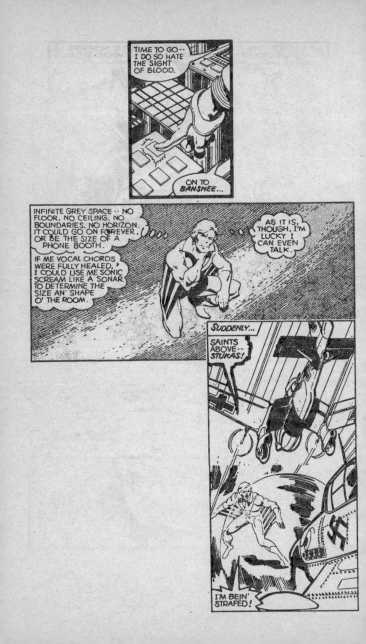

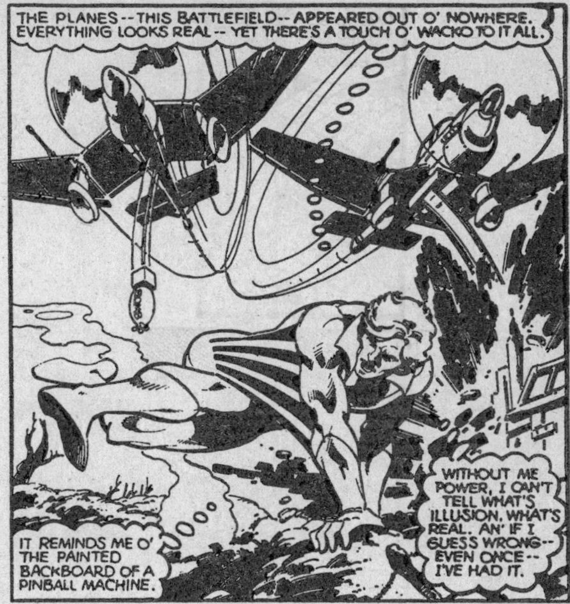
THE PLANES--THIS BATTLEFIELD--APPEARED OUT O' NOWHERE. EVERYTHING LOOKS REAL--YET THERE'S A TOUCH O' WACKO TO IT ALL.
IT REMINDS ME O' THE PAINTED BACKBOARD OF A PINBALL MACHINE.
WITHOUT ME POWER, I CAN'T TELL WHAT'S ILLUSION. WHAT'S REAL. AN' IF I GUESS WRONG--EVEN ONCE--I'VE HAD IT.

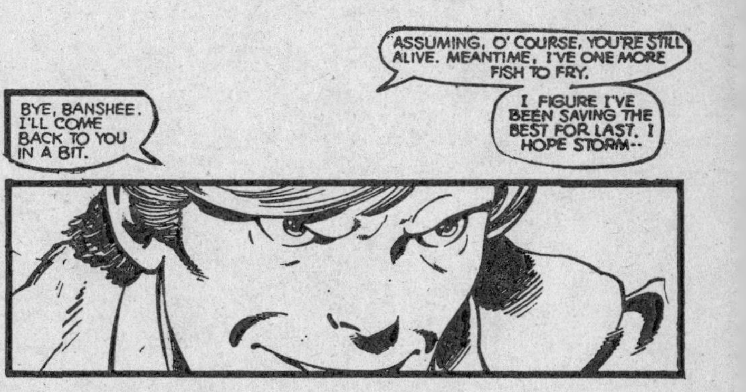
BYE, BANSHEE. I'LL COME BACK TO YOU IN A BIT.
ASSUMING, O' COURSE, YOU'RE STILL ALIVE. MEANTIME, I'VE ONE MORE FISH TO FRY.
I FIGURE I'VE BEEN SAVING THE BEST FOR LAST. I HOPE STORM--

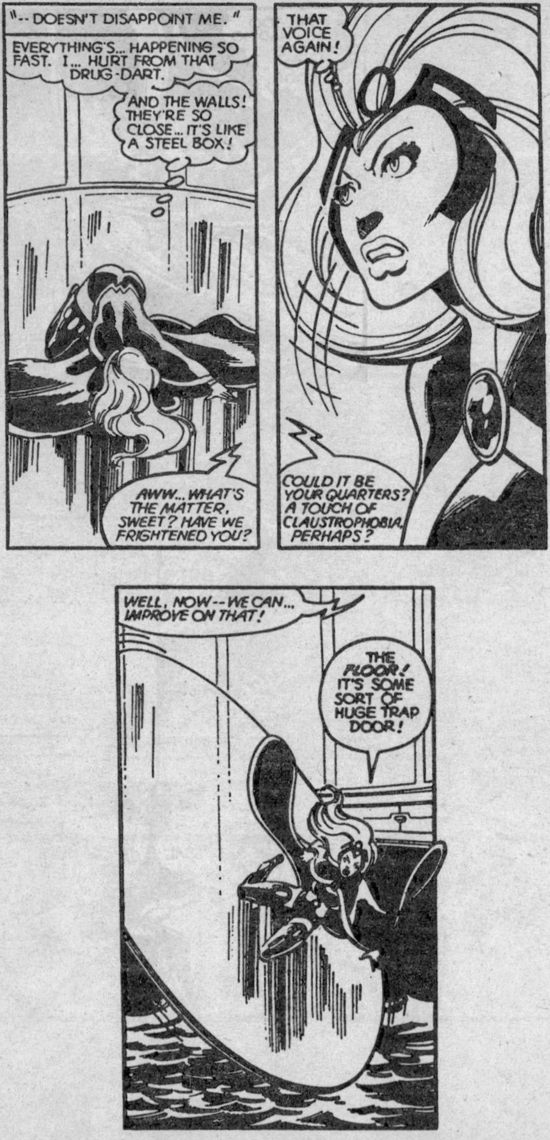
"-- DOESN'T DISAPPOINT ME."
EVERYTHING'S... HAPPENING SO FAST. I... HURT FROM THAT DRUG-DART.
AND THE WALLS! THEY'RE SO CLOSE... IT'S LIKE A STEEL BOX!
AWW... WHAT'S THE MATTER, SWEET? HAVE WE FRIGHTENED YOU?
THAT VOICE AGAIN!
COULD IT BE YOUR QUARTERS? A TOUCH OF CLAUSTROPHOBIA, PERHAPS?
WELL, NOW--WE CAN... IMPROVE ON THAT!
THE FLOOR! IT'S SOME SORT OF HUGE TRAP DOOR!

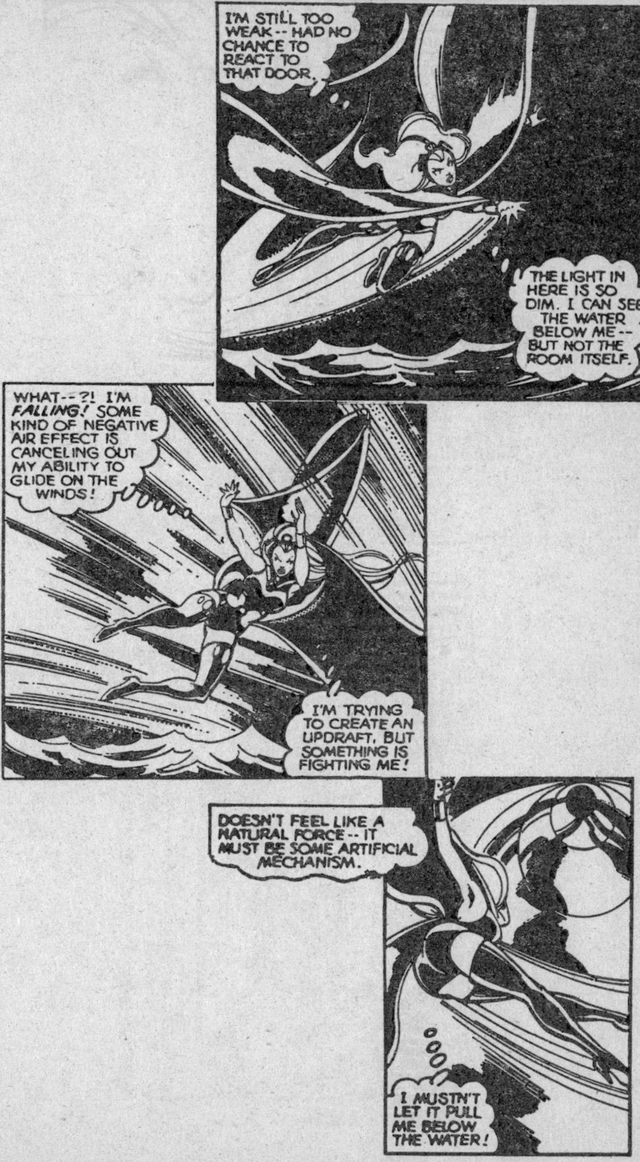
I'M STILL TOO WEAK-- HAD NO CHANCE TO REACT TO THAT DOOR.
THE LIGHT IN HERE IS SO DIM. I CAN SEE THE WATER BELOW ME-- BUT NOT THE ROOM ITSELF.
WHAT--?! I'M FALLING! SOME KIND OF NEGATIVE AIR EFFECT IS CANCELING OUT MY ABILITY TO GLIDE ON THE WINDS!
I'M TRYING TO CREATE AN UPDRAFT, BUT SOMETHING IS FIGHTING ME!
DOESN'T FEEL LIKE A NATURAL FORCE-- IT MUST BE SOME ARTIFICIAL MECHANISM.
I MUSTN'T LET IT PULL ME BELOW THE WATER!

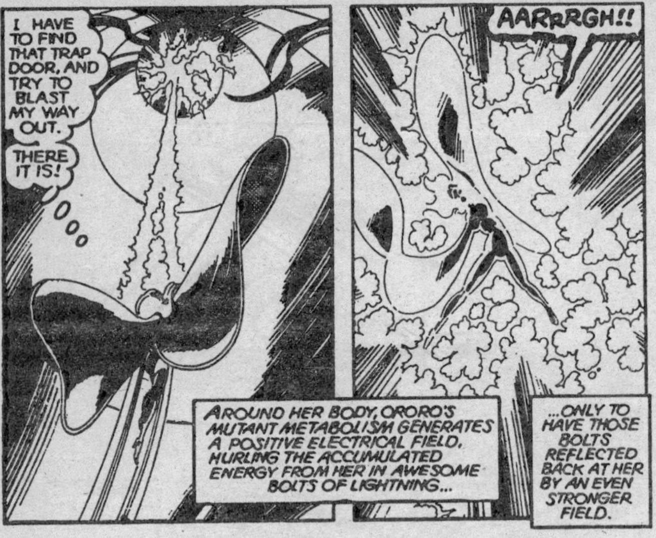
I HAVE TO FIND THAT TRAP DOOR, AND TRY TO BLAST MY WAY OUT.
THERE IT IS!
AARRRGH!!
AROUND HER BODY, ORORO'S MUTANT METABOLISM GENERATES A POSITIVE ELECTRICAL FIELD, HURLING THE ACCUMULATED ENERGY FROM HER IN AWESOME BOLTS OF LIGHTNING...
...ONLY TO HAVE THOSE BOLTS REFLECTED BACK AT HER BY AN EVEN STRONGER FIELD.

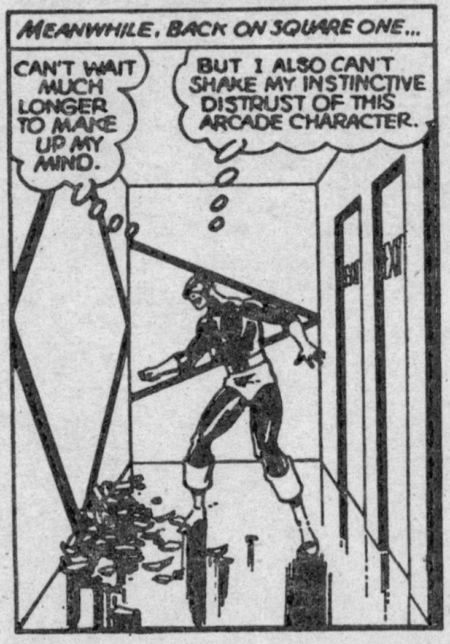
MEANWHILE, BACK ON SQUARE ONE...
CAN'T WAIT MUCH LONGER TO MAKE UP MY MIND.
BUT I ALSO CAN'T SHAKE MY INSTINCTIVE DISTRUST OF THIS ARCADE CHARACTER.

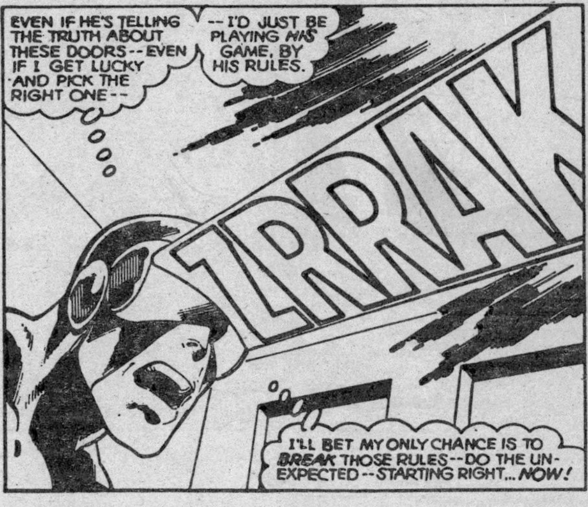
EVEN IF HE'S TELLING THE TRUTH ABOUT THESE DOORS--EVEN IF I GET LUCKY AND PICK THE RIGHT ONE--
--I'D JUST BE PLAYING HIS GAME, BY HIS RULES.
ZRRAK
I'LL BET MY ONLY CHANCE IS TO BREAK THOSE RULES--DO THE UN-EXPECTED--STARTING RIGHT...NOW!

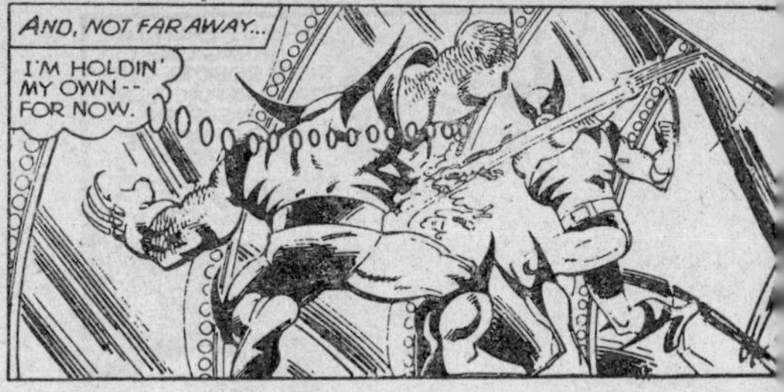
AND, NOT FAR AWAY...
I'M HOLDIN' MY OWN -- FOR NOW.

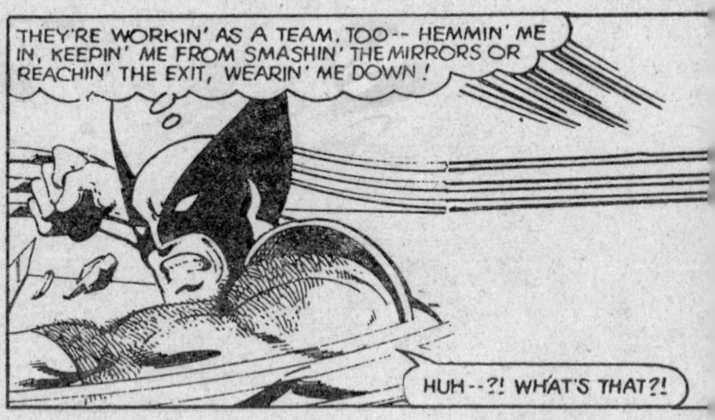
THEY'RE WORKIN' AS A TEAM, TOO-- HEMMIN' ME IN, KEEPIN' ME FROM SMASHIN' THE MIRRORS OR REACHIN' THE EXIT, WEARIN' ME DOWN!
HUH --?! WHAT'S THAT?!

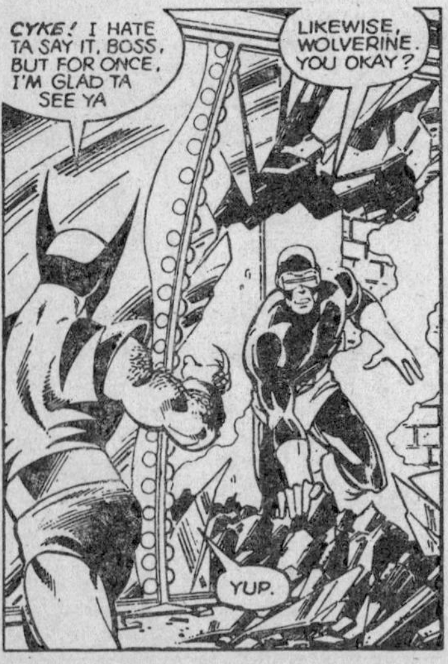
CYKE! I HATE TA SAY IT, BOSS, BUT FOR ONCE, I'M GLAD TA SEE YA
LIKEWISE, WOLVERINE. YOU OKAY?
YUP.

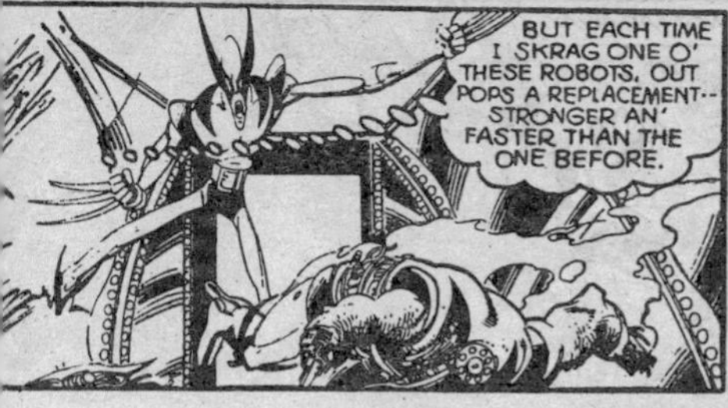
BUT EACH TIME I SKRAG ONE O' THESE ROBOTS, OUT POPS A REPLACEMENT-- STRONGER AN' FASTER THAN THE ONE BEFORE.

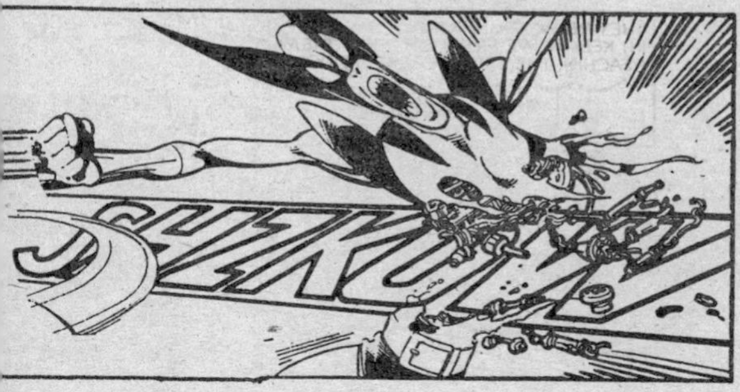
SHUKK

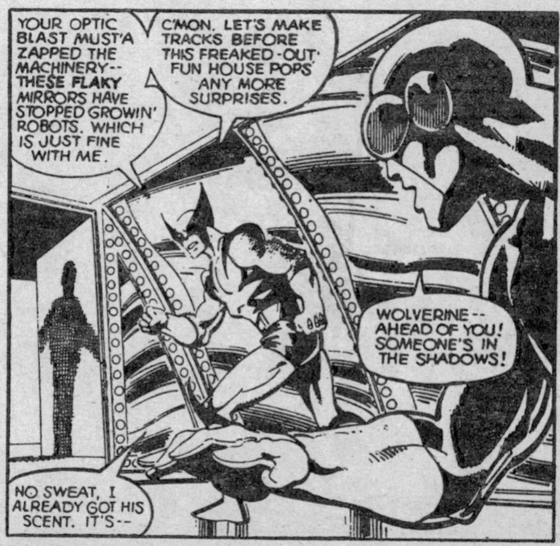
YOUR OPTIC BLAST MUST'A ZAPPED THE MACHINERY-- THESE **FLAKY** MIRRORS HAVE STOPPED GROWIN' ROBOTS. WHICH IS JUST FINE WITH ME.
C'MON. LET'S MAKE TRACKS BEFORE THIS FREAKED-OUT FUN HOUSE POPS ANY MORE SURPRISES.
WOLVERINE-- AHEAD OF YOU! SOMEONE'S IN THE SHADOWS!
NO SWEAT, I ALREADY GOT HIS SCENT. IT'S--

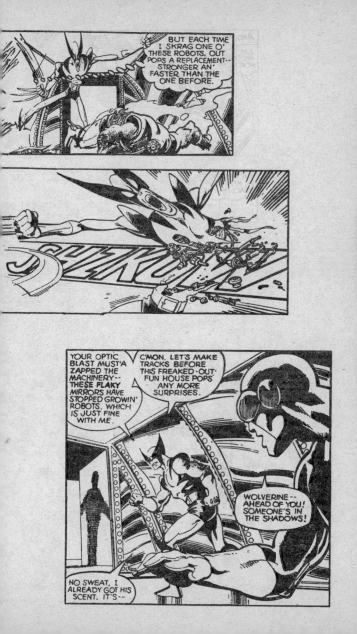

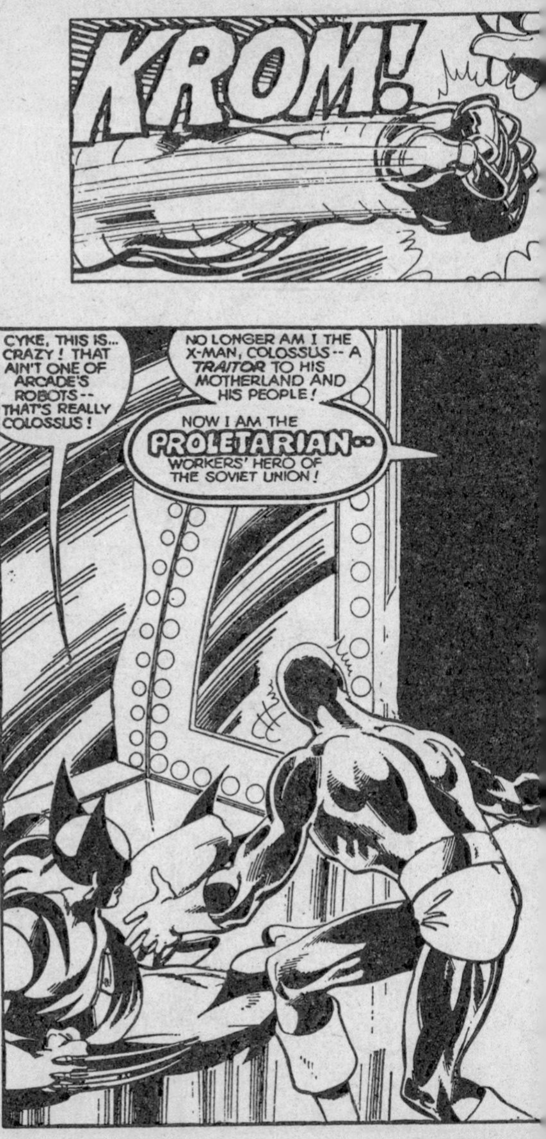
KROM!
CYKE, THIS IS... CRAZY! THAT AIN'T ONE OF ARCADE'S ROBOTS -- THAT'S REALLY COLOSSUS!
NO LONGER AM I THE X-MAN, COLOSSUS -- A TRAITOR TO HIS MOTHERLAND AND HIS PEOPLE!
NOW I AM THE PROLETARIAN -- WORKERS' HERO OF THE SOVIET UNION!

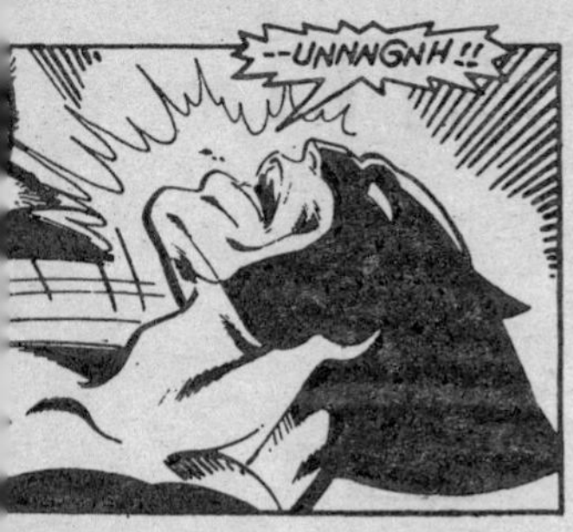
--UNNNGNH!!

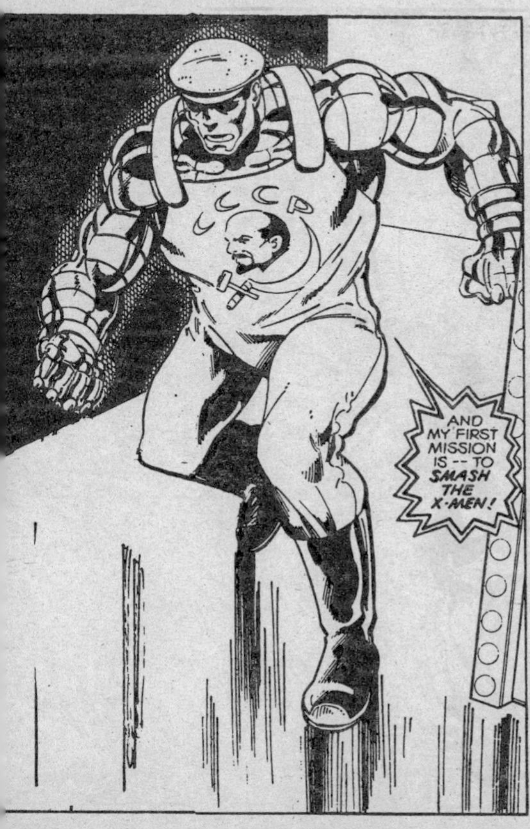
UCCP
AND MY FIRST MISSION IS -- TO SMASH THE X-MEN!

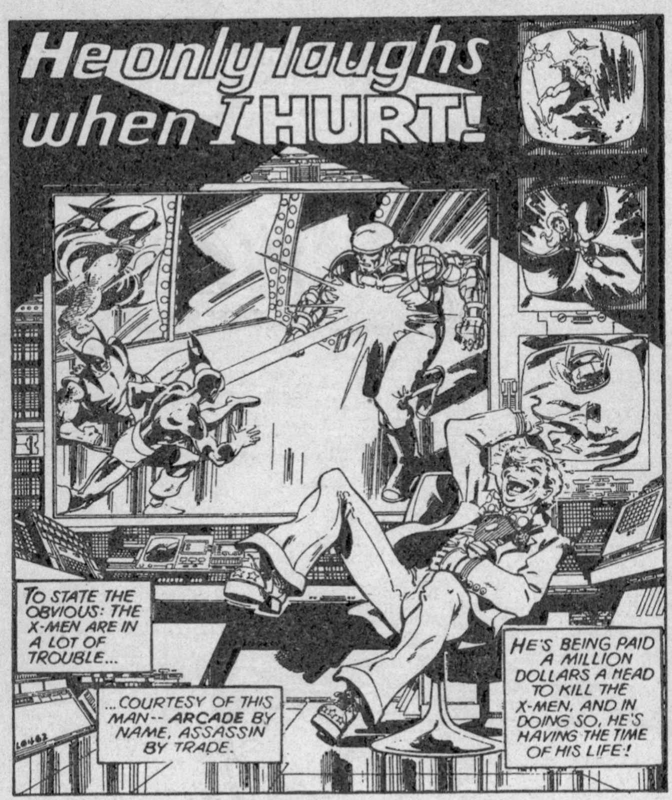
He only laughs when I HURT!
TO STATE THE OBVIOUS: THE X-MEN ARE IN A LOT OF TROUBLE...
...COURTESY OF THIS MAN-- ARCADE BY NAME, ASSASSIN BY TRADE.
HE'S BEING PAID A MILLION DOLLARS A HEAD TO KILL THE X-MEN, AND IN DOING SO, HE'S HAVING THE TIME OF HIS LIFE!

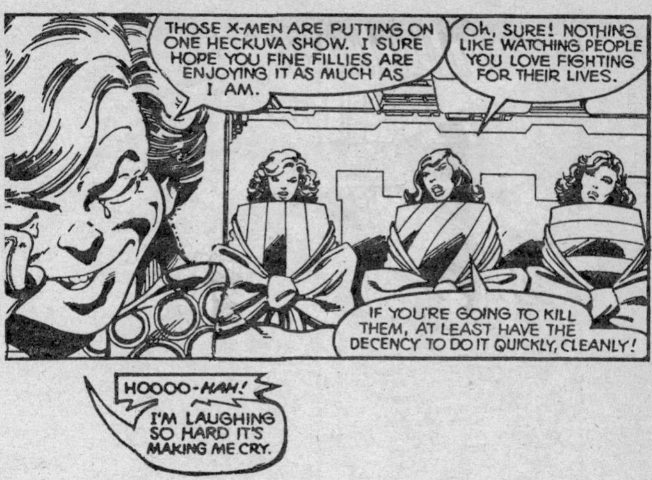
THOSE X-MEN ARE PUTTING ON ONE HECKUVA SHOW. I SURE HOPE YOU FINE FILLIES ARE ENJOYING IT AS MUCH AS I AM.
Oh, SURE! NOTHING LIKE WATCHING PEOPLE YOU LOVE FIGHTING FOR THEIR LIVES.
IF YOU'RE GOING TO KILL THEM, AT LEAST HAVE THE DECENCY TO DO IT QUICKLY, CLEANLY!
HOOOO-*HAH!*
I'M LAUGHING SO HARD IT'S MAKING ME CRY.

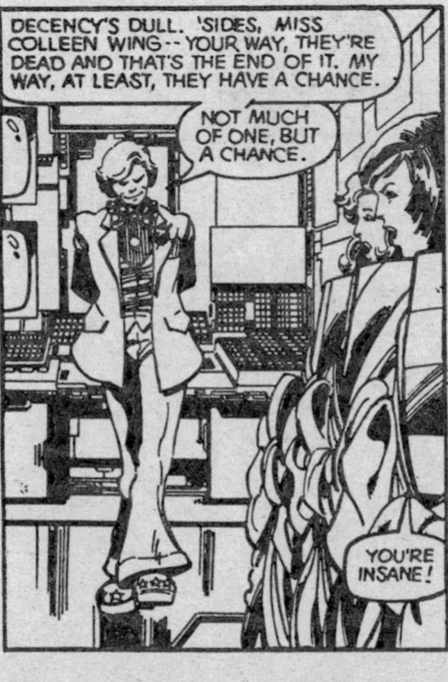
DECENCY'S DULL. 'SIDES, MISS COLLEEN WING-- YOUR WAY, THEY'RE DEAD AND THAT'S THE END OF IT. MY WAY, AT LEAST, THEY HAVE A CHANCE.
NOT MUCH OF ONE, BUT A CHANCE.
YOU'RE INSANE!

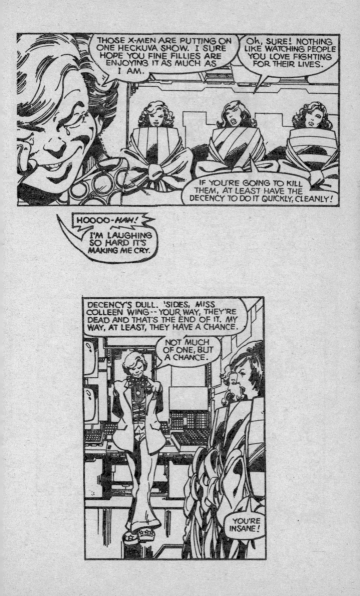

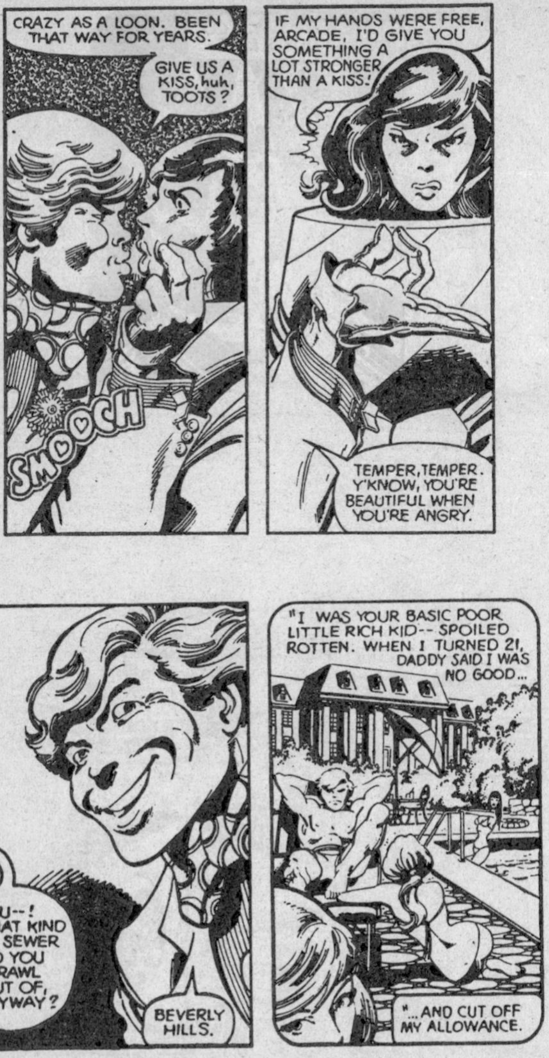

CRAZY AS A LOON. BEEN THAT WAY FOR YEARS.
GIVE US A KISS, huh, TOOTS?
SMOOCH
IF MY HANDS WERE FREE, ARCADE, I'D GIVE YOU SOMETHING A LOT STRONGER THAN A KISS!
TEMPER, TEMPER. Y'KNOW, YOU'RE BEAUTIFUL WHEN YOU'RE ANGRY.
YOU--! WHAT KIND OF SEWER DID YOU CRAWL OUT OF, ANYWAY?
BEVERLY HILLS.
"I WAS YOUR BASIC POOR LITTLE RICH KID-- SPOILED ROTTEN. WHEN I TURNED 21, DADDY SAID I WAS NO GOOD...
"...AND CUT OFF MY ALLOWANCE.

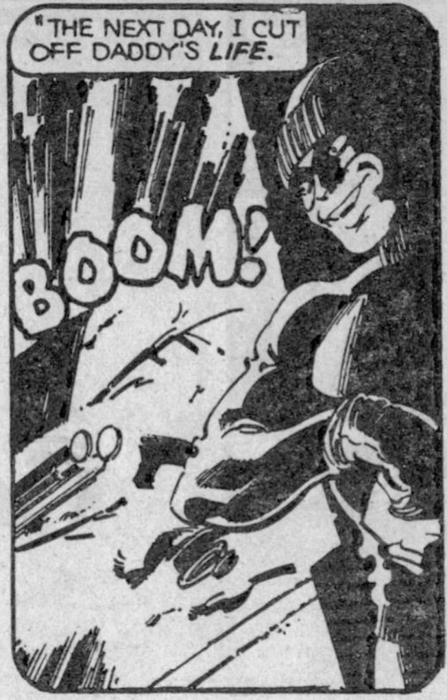
"THE NEXT DAY, I CUT OFF DADDY'S *LIFE*.
BOOM!

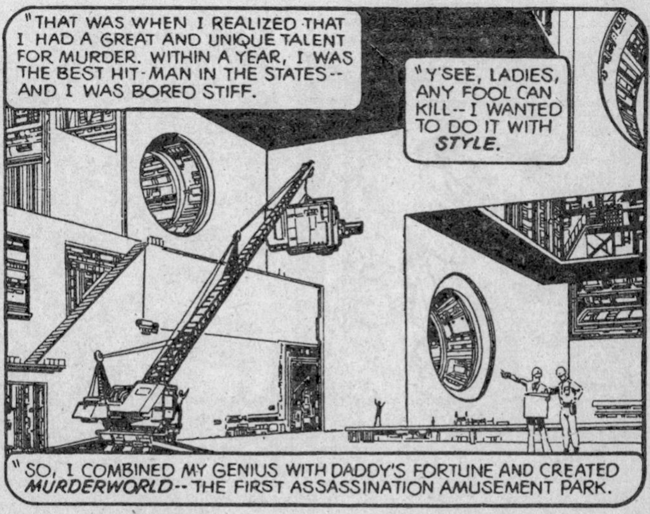
"THAT WAS WHEN I REALIZED THAT I HAD A GREAT AND UNIQUE TALENT FOR MURDER. WITHIN A YEAR, I WAS THE BEST HIT-MAN IN THE STATES-- AND I WAS BORED STIFF.
"Y'SEE, LADIES, ANY FOOL CAN KILL--I WANTED TO DO IT WITH *STYLE*.
"SO, I COMBINED MY GENIUS WITH DADDY'S FORTUNE AND CREATED *MURDERWORLD*-- THE FIRST ASSASSINATION AMUSEMENT PARK.

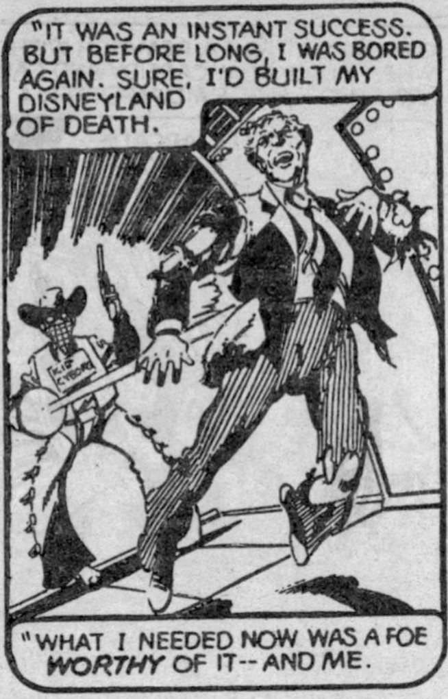
"IT WAS AN INSTANT SUCCESS. BUT BEFORE LONG, I WAS BORED AGAIN. SURE, I'D BUILT MY DISNEYLAND OF DEATH.
"WHAT I NEEDED NOW WAS A FOE *WORTHY* OF IT--AND ME.

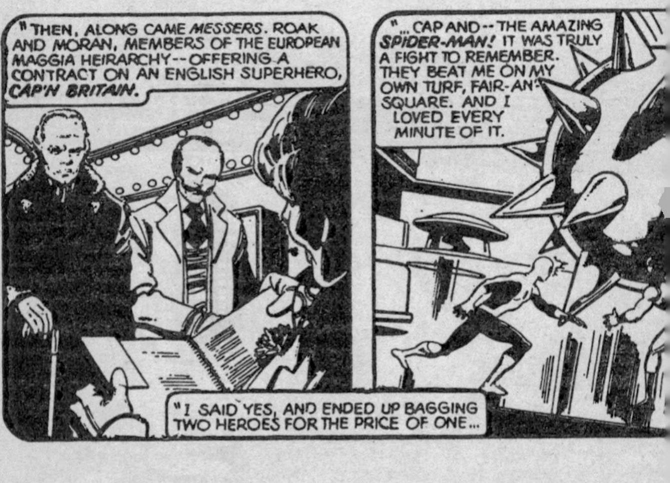
"THEN, ALONG CAME *MESSERS*. ROAK AND *MORAN*, MEMBERS OF THE EUROPEAN MAGGIA HEIRARCHY--OFFERING A CONTRACT ON AN ENGLISH SUPERHERO, *CAP'N BRITAIN*.
"I SAID YES, AND ENDED UP BAGGING TWO HEROES FOR THE PRICE OF ONE...
"...CAP AND--THE AMAZING *SPIDER-MAN!* IT WAS TRULY A FIGHT TO REMEMBER. THEY BEAT ME ON MY OWN TURF, FAIR-AN'-SQUARE. AND I LOVED EVERY MINUTE OF IT.

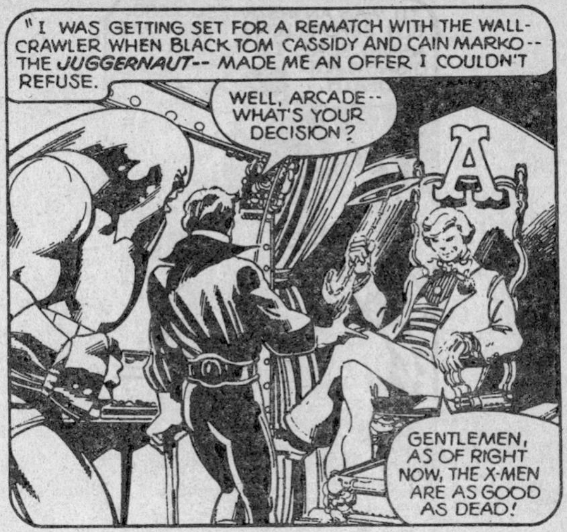
"I WAS GETTING SET FOR A REMATCH WITH THE WALL-CRAWLER WHEN BLACK TOM CASSIDY AND CAIN MARKO -- THE JUGGERNAUT-- MADE ME AN OFFER I COULDN'T REFUSE.
WELL, ARCADE -- WHAT'S YOUR DECISION?
GENTLEMEN, AS OF RIGHT NOW, THE X-MEN ARE AS GOOD AS DEAD!

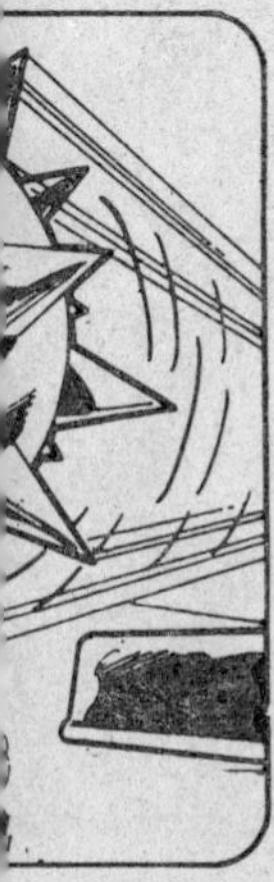

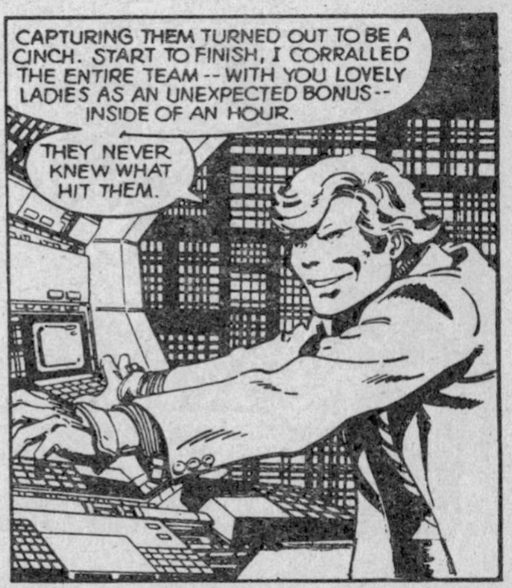
CAPTURING THEM TURNED OUT TO BE A CINCH. START TO FINISH, I CORRALLED THE ENTIRE TEAM -- WITH YOU LOVELY LADIES AS AN UNEXPECTED BONUS -- INSIDE OF AN HOUR.
THEY NEVER KNEW WHAT HIT THEM.

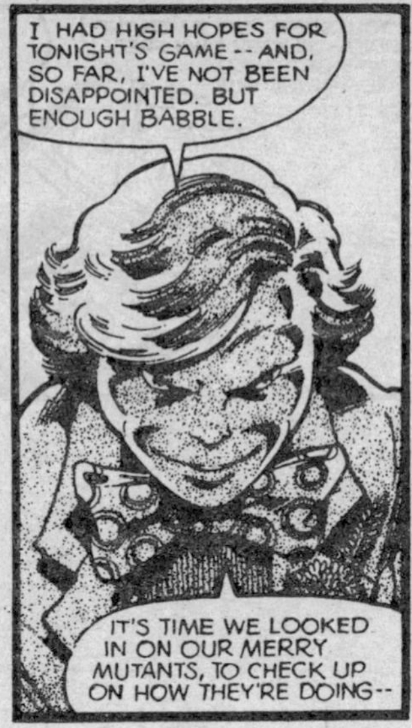
I HAD HIGH HOPES FOR TONIGHT'S GAME -- AND, SO FAR, I'VE NOT BEEN DISAPPOINTED. BUT ENOUGH BABBLE.
IT'S TIME WE LOOKED IN ON OUR MERRY MUTANTS, TO CHECK UP ON HOW THEY'RE DOING--

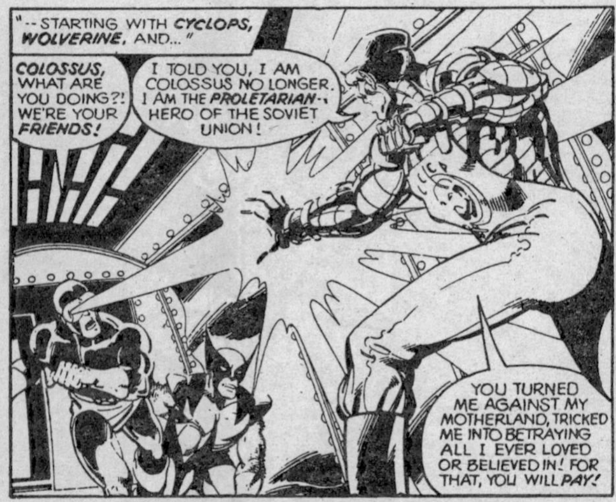
"--STARTING WITH CYCLOPS, WOLVERINE, AND..."
COLOSSUS, WHAT ARE YOU DOING?! WE'RE YOUR FRIENDS!
I TOLD YOU, I AM COLOSSUS NO LONGER. I AM THE PROLETARIAN--HERO OF THE SOVIET UNION!
YOU TURNED ME AGAINST MY MOTHERLAND, TRICKED ME INTO BETRAYING ALL I EVER LOVED OR BELIEVED IN! FOR THAT, YOU WILL PAY!

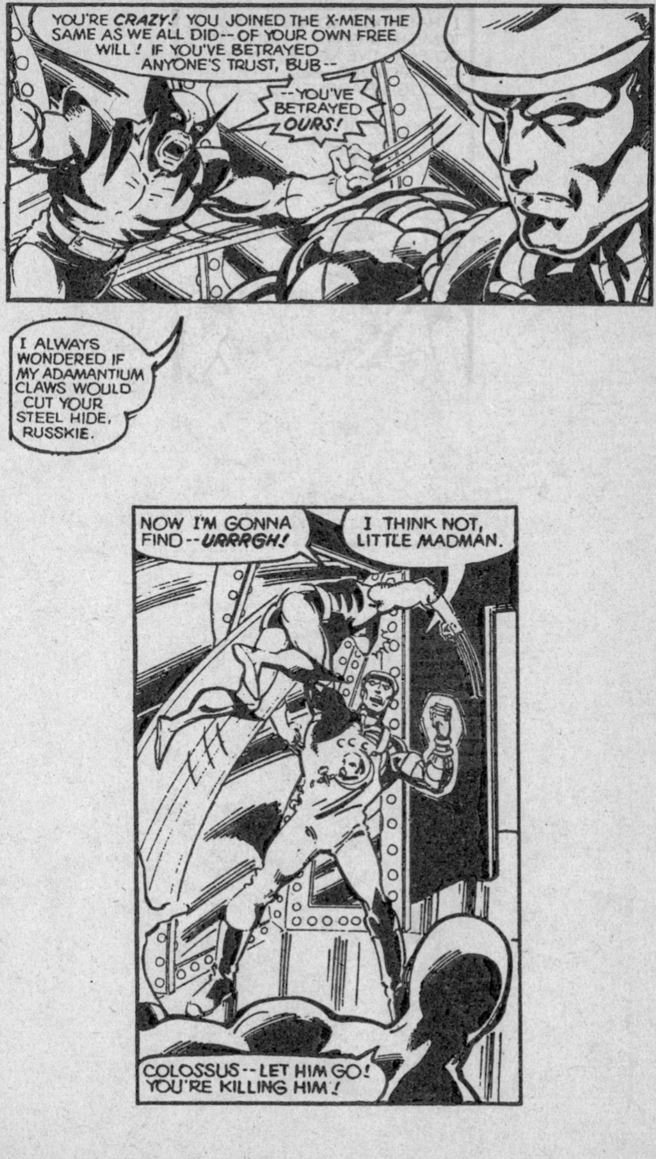

YOU'RE CRAZY! YOU JOINED THE X-MEN THE SAME AS WE ALL DID--OF YOUR OWN FREE WILL! IF YOU'VE BETRAYED ANYONE'S TRUST, BUB--
--YOU'VE BETRAYED OURS!
I ALWAYS WONDERED IF MY ADAMANTIUM CLAWS WOULD CUT YOUR STEEL HIDE, RUSSKIE.
NOW I'M GONNA FIND--URRRGH!
I THINK NOT, LITTLE MADMAN.
COLOSSUS--LET HIM GO! YOU'RE KILLING HIM!

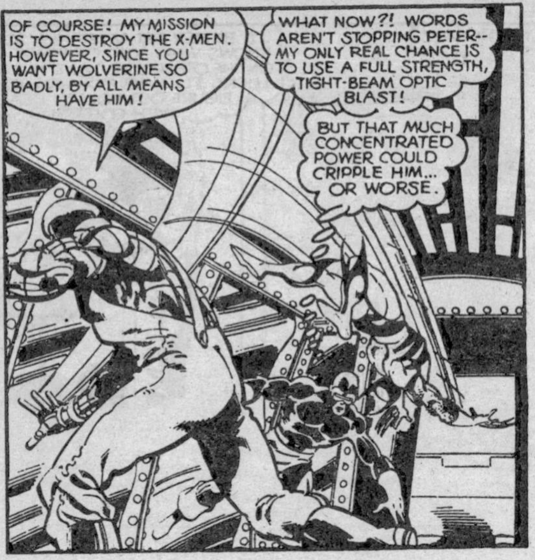
OF COURSE! MY MISSION IS TO DESTROY THE X-MEN. HOWEVER, SINCE YOU WANT WOLVERINE SO BADLY, BY ALL MEANS HAVE HIM!
WHAT NOW?! WORDS AREN'T STOPPING PETER-- MY ONLY REAL CHANCE IS TO USE A FULL STRENGTH, TIGHT-BEAM OPTIC BLAST!
BUT THAT MUCH CONCENTRATED POWER COULD CRIPPLE HIM... OR WORSE.

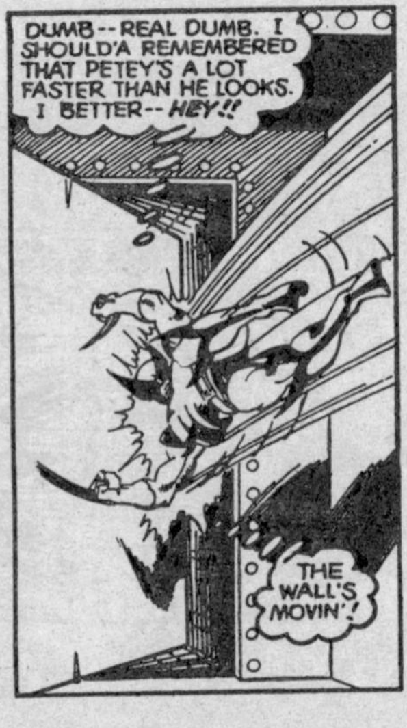
DUMB--REAL DUMB. I SHOULD'A REMEMBERED THAT PETEY'S A LOT FASTER THAN HE LOOKS. I BETTER--HEY!!
THE WALL'S MOVIN'!

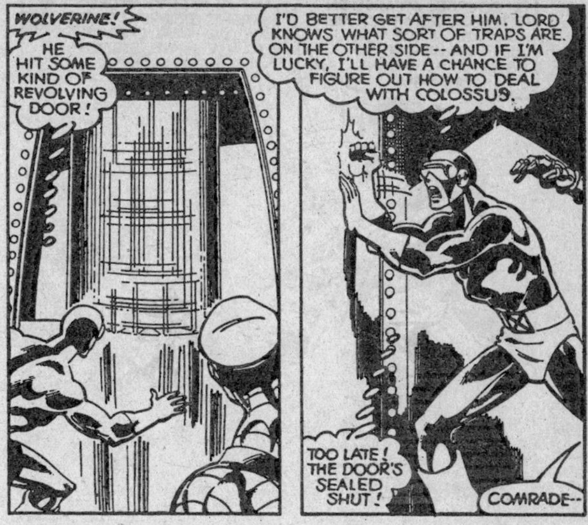
WOLVERINE!
HE HIT SOME KIND OF REVOLVING DOOR!
I'D BETTER GET AFTER HIM. LORD KNOWS WHAT SORT OF TRAPS ARE ON THE OTHER SIDE-- AND IF I'M LUCKY, I'LL HAVE A CHANCE TO FIGURE OUT HOW TO DEAL WITH COLOSSUS.
TOO LATE! THE DOOR'S SEALED SHUT!
COMRADE--

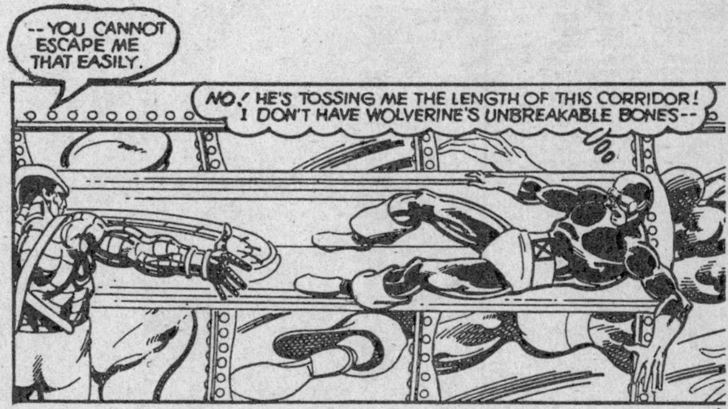
--YOU CANNOT ESCAPE ME THAT EASILY.
NO! HE'S TOSSING ME THE LENGTH OF THIS CORRIDOR! I DON'T HAVE WOLVERINE'S UNBREAKABLE BONES--

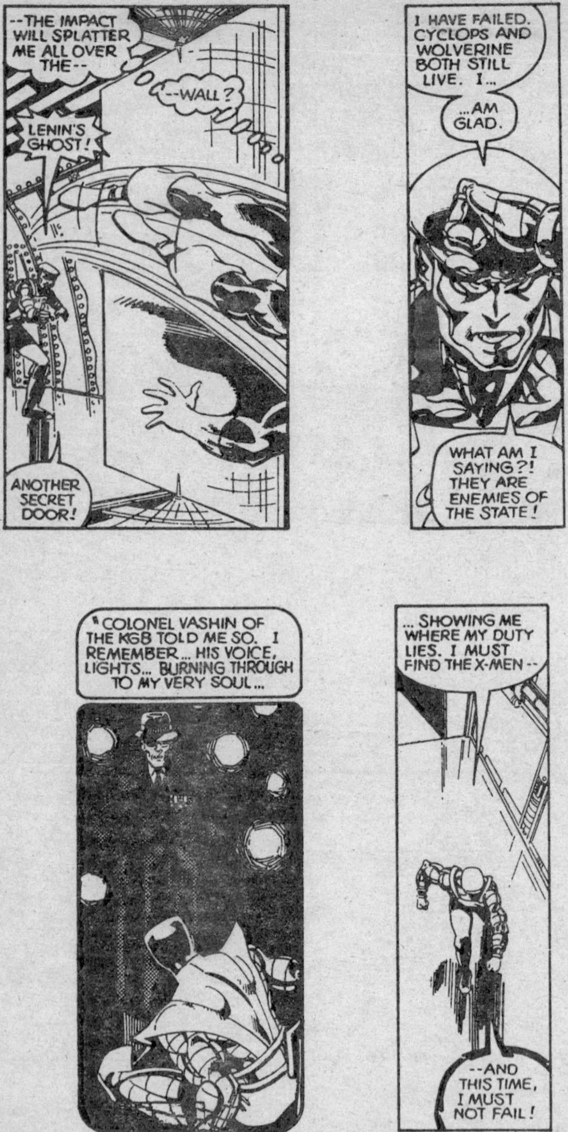

--THE IMPACT WILL SPLATTER ME ALL OVER THE--
--WALL?
LENIN'S GHOST!
ANOTHER SECRET DOOR!
I HAVE FAILED. CYCLOPS AND WOLVERINE BOTH STILL LIVE. I...
...AM GLAD.
WHAT AM I SAYING?! THEY ARE ENEMIES OF THE STATE!
"COLONEL VASHIN OF THE KGB TOLD ME SO. I REMEMBER... HIS VOICE, LIGHTS... BURNING THROUGH TO MY VERY SOUL...
... SHOWING ME WHERE MY DUTY LIES. I MUST FIND THE X-MEN --
--AND THIS TIME, I MUST NOT FAIL!

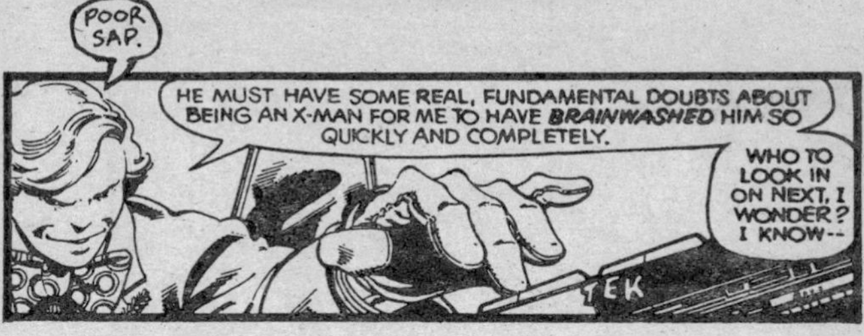
POOR SAP.
HE MUST HAVE SOME REAL, FUNDAMENTAL DOUBTS ABOUT BEING AN X-MAN FOR ME TO HAVE BRAINWASHED HIM SO QUICKLY AND COMPLETELY.
WHO TO LOOK IN ON NEXT, I WONDER? I KNOW--
TEK

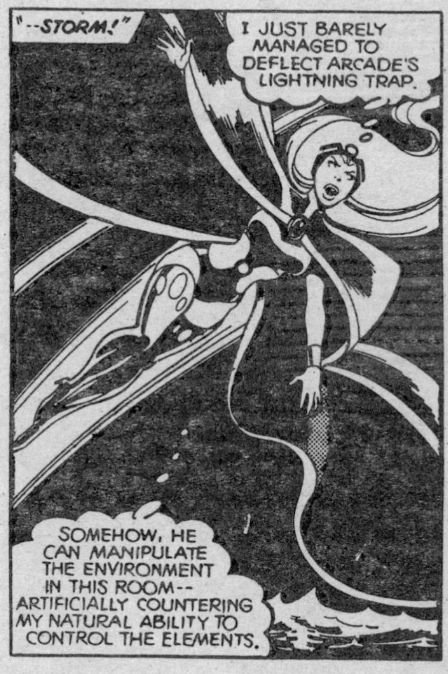
"--STORM!"
I JUST BARELY MANAGED TO DEFLECT ARCADE'S LIGHTNING TRAP.
SOMEHOW, HE CAN MANIPULATE THE ENVIRONMENT IN THIS ROOM-- ARTIFICIALLY COUNTERING MY NATURAL ABILITY TO CONTROL THE ELEMENTS.

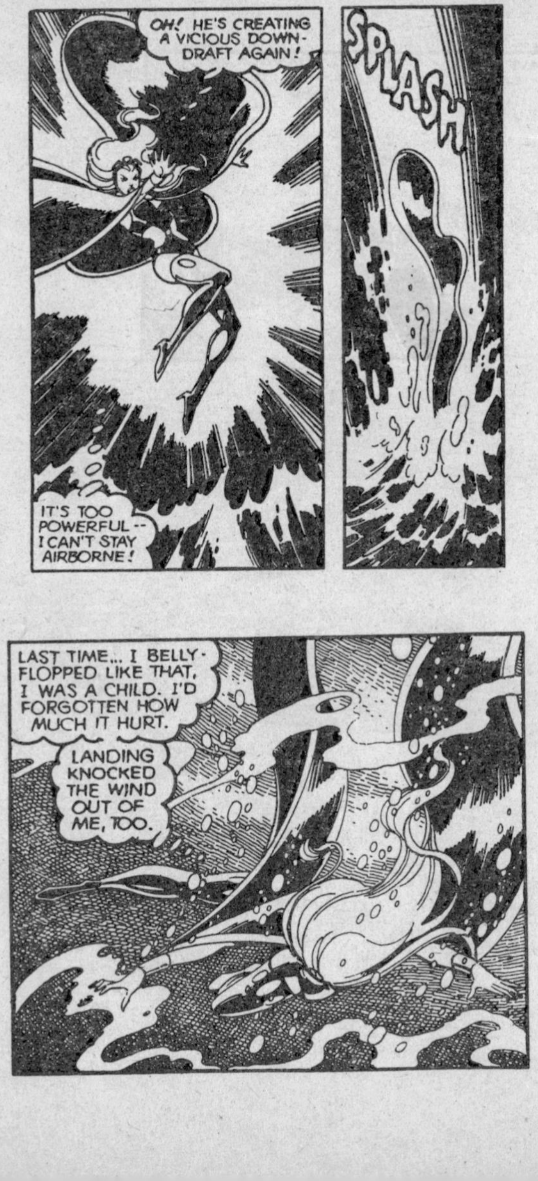
OH! HE'S CREATING A VICIOUS DOWN-DRAFT AGAIN!
IT'S TOO POWERFUL -- I CAN'T STAY AIRBORNE!
SPLASH
LAST TIME... I BELLY-FLOPPED LIKE THAT, I WAS A CHILD. I'D FORGOTTEN HOW MUCH IT HURT.
LANDING KNOCKED THE WIND OUT OF ME, TOO.

I HAVE TO GET BACK TO THE SURFACE.
WATER'S A MUCH HEAVIER MEDIUM THAN AIR -- IT'S MUCH HARDER FOR ME TO MANIPULATE. BUT AS SOON AS I CATCH MY BREATH, I'LL...

NO -- oh, NO! THE WATER LEVEL'S RISEN ALMOST TO THE CEILING!
ANOTHER FEW INCHES, AND I'LL DROWN!

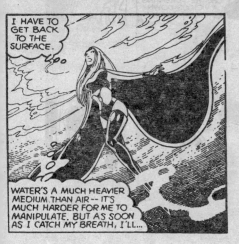

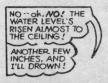

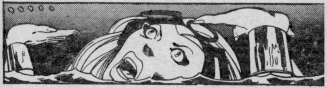

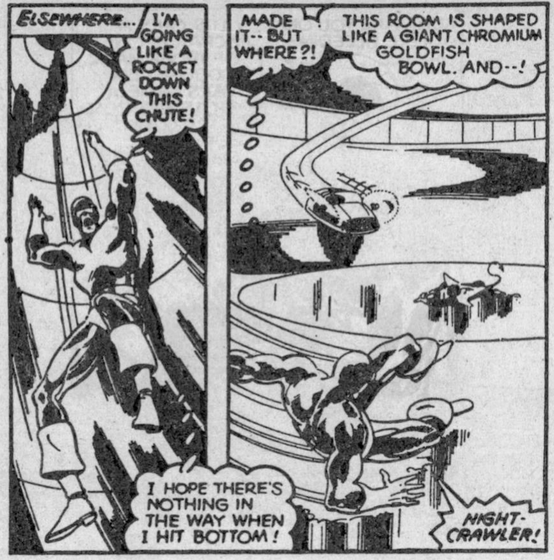
ELSEWHERE...
I'M GOING LIKE A ROCKET DOWN THIS CHUTE!
I HOPE THERE'S NOTHING IN THE WAY WHEN I HIT BOTTOM!
MADE IT-- BUT WHERE?!
THIS ROOM IS SHAPED LIKE A GIANT CHROMIUM GOLDFISH BOWL. AND--!
NIGHT-CRAWLER!

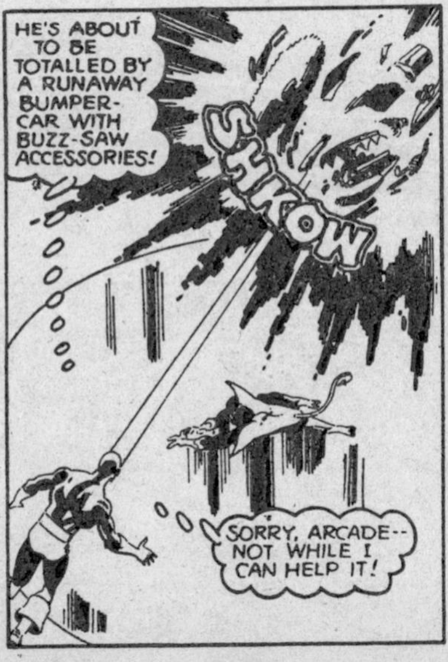
HE'S ABOUT TO BE TOTALLED BY A RUNAWAY BUMPER-CAR WITH BUZZ-SAW ACCESSORIES!
SHKOW
SORRY, ARCADE-- NOT WHILE I CAN HELP IT!

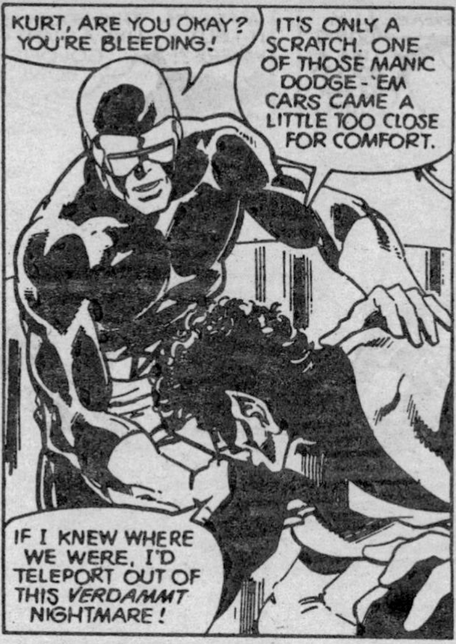
KURT, ARE YOU OKAY? YOU'RE BLEEDING!
IT'S ONLY A SCRATCH. ONE OF THOSE MANIC DODGE-'EM CARS CAME A LITTLE TOO CLOSE FOR COMFORT.
IF I KNEW WHERE WE WERE, I'D TELEPORT OUT OF THIS *VERDAMMT* NIGHTMARE!

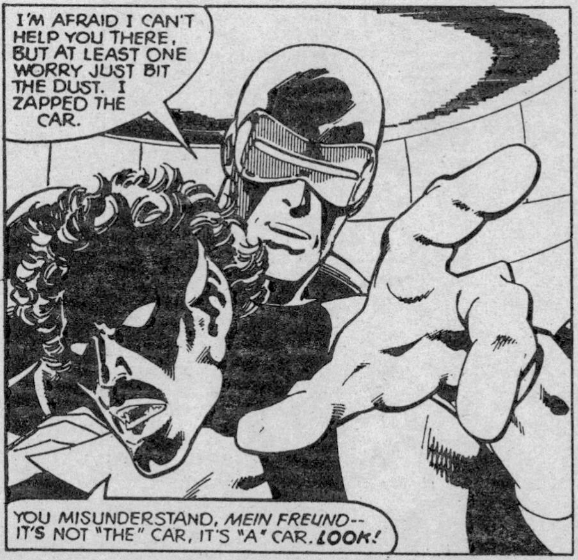
I'M AFRAID I CAN'T HELP YOU THERE, BUT AT LEAST ONE WORRY JUST BIT THE DUST. I ZAPPED THE CAR.
YOU MISUNDERSTAND, *MEIN FREUND*-- IT'S NOT "THE" CAR, IT'S "A" CAR. ***LOOK!***

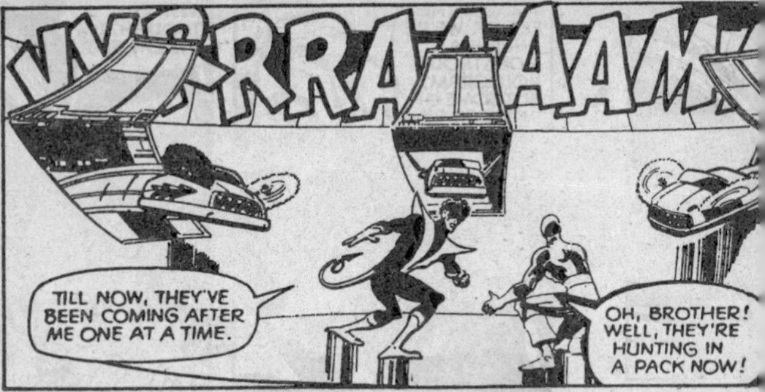
VVRRRAAAAM
TILL NOW, THEY'VE BEEN COMING AFTER ME ONE AT A TIME.
OH, BROTHER! WELL, THEY'RE HUNTING IN A PACK NOW!

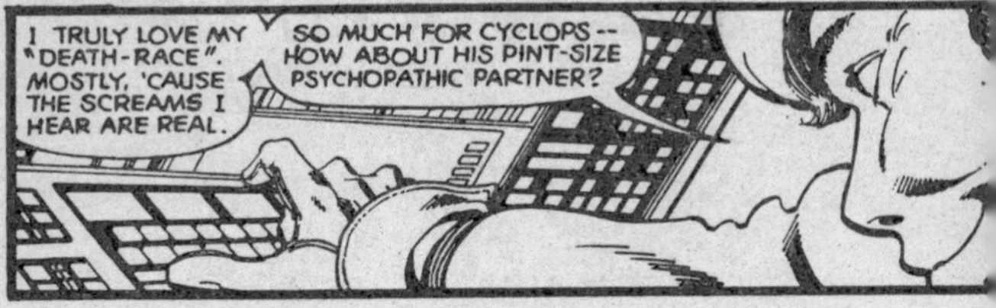
I TRULY LOVE MY "DEATH-RACE". MOSTLY, 'CAUSE THE SCREAMS I HEAR ARE REAL.
SO MUCH FOR CYCLOPS -- HOW ABOUT HIS PINT-SIZE PSYCHOPATHIC PARTNER?

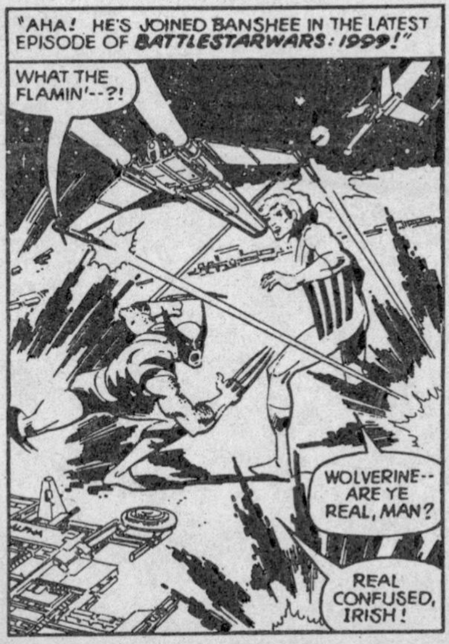
"AHA! HE'S JOINED BANSHEE IN THE LATEST EPISODE OF BATTLESTARWARS: 1999!"
WHAT THE FLAMIN'--?!
WOLVERINE--ARE YE REAL, MAN?
REAL CONFUSED, IRISH!

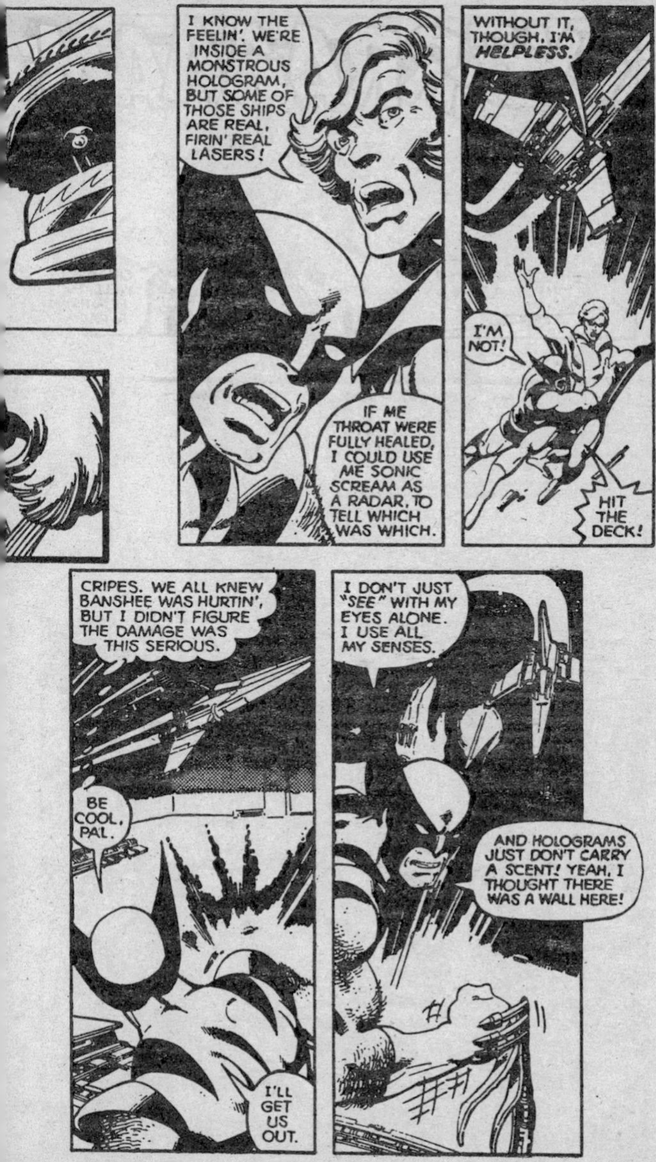
I KNOW THE FEELIN'. WE'RE INSIDE A MONSTROUS HOLOGRAM, BUT SOME OF THOSE SHIPS ARE REAL, FIRIN' REAL LASERS!
IF ME THROAT WERE FULLY HEALED, I COULD USE ME SONIC SCREAM AS A RADAR, TO TELL WHICH WAS WHICH.
WITHOUT IT, THOUGH, I'M HELPLESS.
I'M NOT!
HIT THE DECK!
CRIPES. WE ALL KNEW BANSHEE WAS HURTIN', BUT I DIDN'T FIGURE THE DAMAGE WAS THIS SERIOUS.
BE COOL, PAL.
I'LL GET US OUT.
I DON'T JUST "SEE" WITH MY EYES ALONE. I USE ALL MY SENSES.
AND HOLOGRAMS JUST DON'T CARRY A SCENT! YEAH, I THOUGHT THERE WAS A WALL HERE!

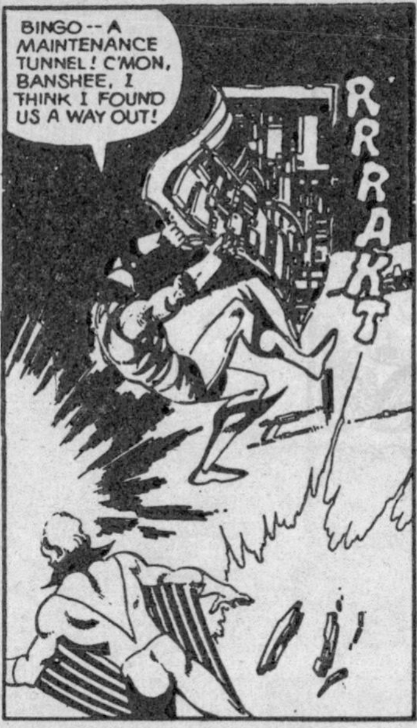
BINGO--A MAINTENANCE TUNNEL! C'MON, BANSHEE, I THINK I FOUND US A WAY OUT!
RRRAKT

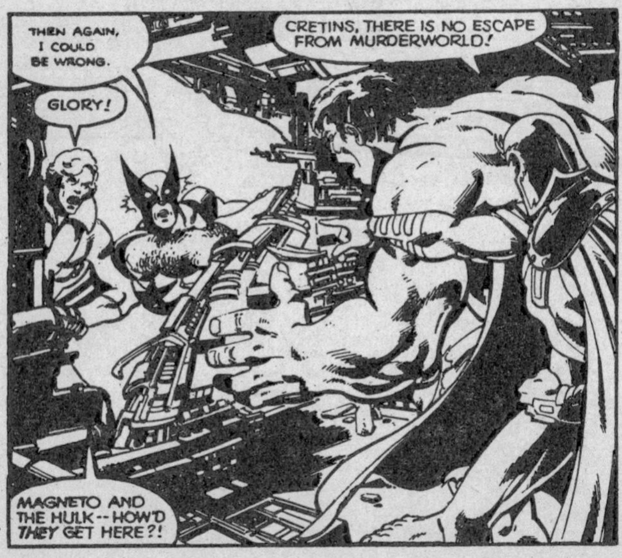
THEN AGAIN, I COULD BE WRONG.
CRETINS, THERE IS NO ESCAPE FROM MURDERWORLD!
GLORY!
MAGNETO AND THE HULK--HOW'D *THEY* GET HERE?!

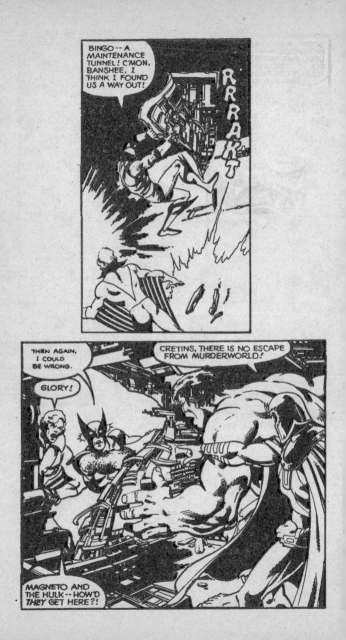

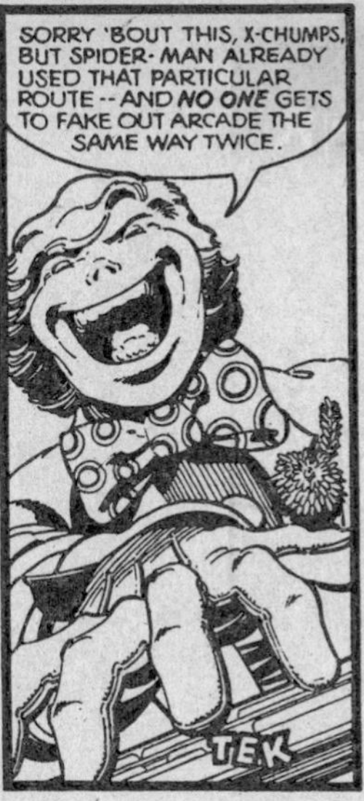
SORRY 'BOUT THIS, X-CHUMPS, BUT SPIDER-MAN ALREADY USED THAT PARTICULAR ROUTE -- AND NO ONE GETS TO FAKE OUT ARCADE THE SAME WAY TWICE.
TEK

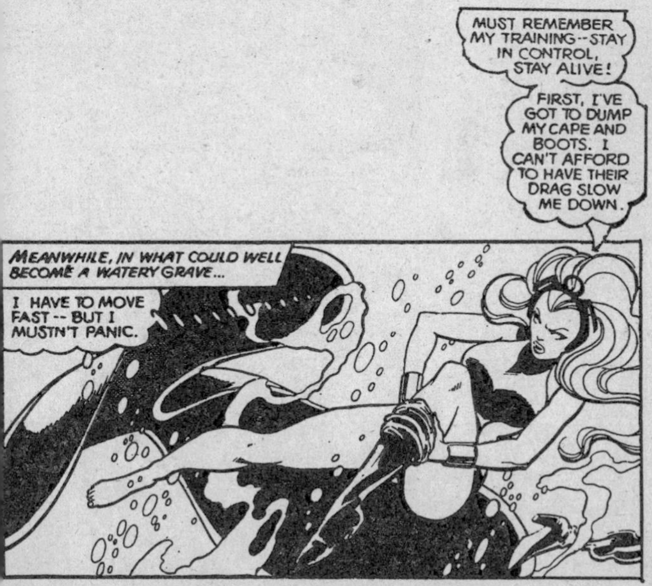
MEANWHILE, IN WHAT COULD WELL BECOME A WATERY GRAVE...
I HAVE TO MOVE FAST -- BUT I MUSTN'T PANIC.
MUST REMEMBER MY TRAINING -- STAY IN CONTROL, STAY ALIVE!
FIRST, I'VE GOT TO DUMP MY CAPE AND BOOTS. I CAN'T AFFORD TO HAVE THEIR DRAG SLOW ME DOWN.

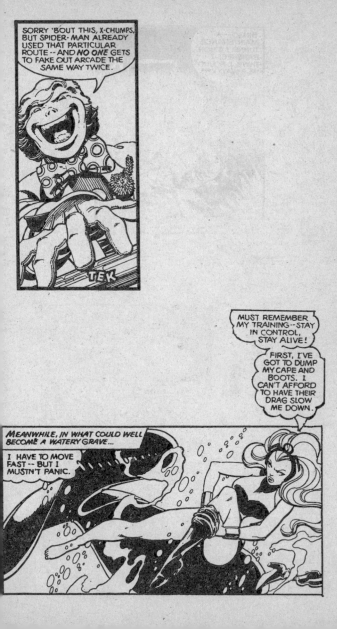

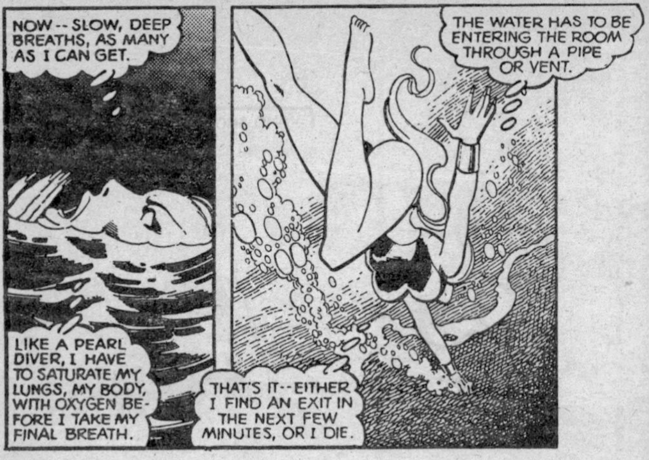
NOW -- SLOW, DEEP BREATHS, AS MANY AS I CAN GET.
LIKE A PEARL DIVER, I HAVE TO SATURATE MY LUNGS, MY BODY, WITH OXYGEN BEFORE I TAKE MY FINAL BREATH.
THE WATER HAS TO BE ENTERING THE ROOM THROUGH A PIPE OR VENT.
THAT'S IT -- EITHER I FIND AN EXIT IN THE NEXT FEW MINUTES, OR I DIE.

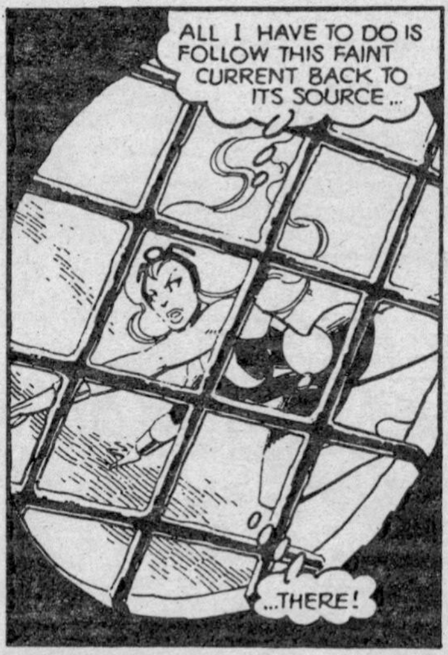
ALL I HAVE TO DO IS FOLLOW THIS FAINT CURRENT BACK TO ITS SOURCE ...
...THERE!

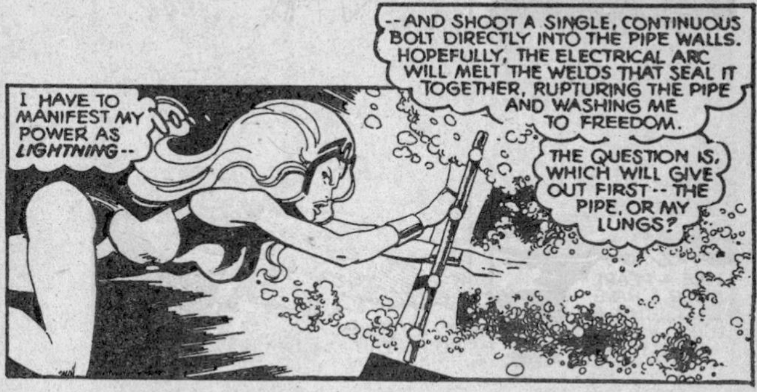
I HAVE TO MANIFEST MY POWER AS *LIGHTNING*--
--AND SHOOT A SINGLE, CONTINUOUS BOLT DIRECTLY INTO THE PIPE WALLS. HOPEFULLY, THE ELECTRICAL ARC WILL MELT THE WELDS THAT SEAL IT TOGETHER, RUPTURING THE PIPE AND WASHING ME TO FREEDOM.
THE QUESTION IS, WHICH WILL GIVE OUT FIRST -- THE PIPE, OR MY LUNGS?

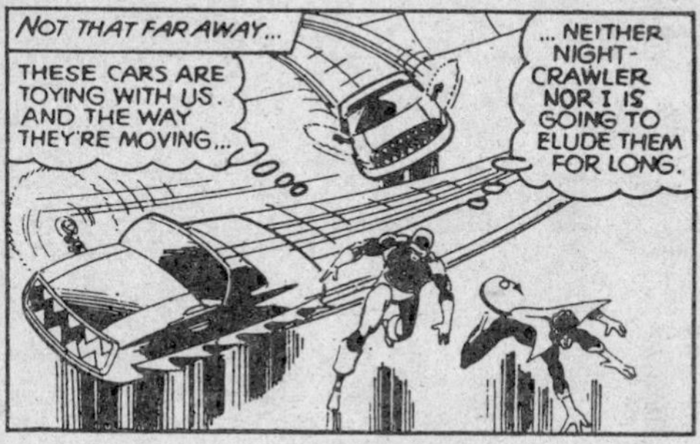
NOT THAT FAR AWAY...
THESE CARS ARE TOYING WITH US. AND THE WAY THEY'RE MOVING...
...NEITHER NIGHT-CRAWLER NOR I IS GOING TO ELUDE THEM FOR LONG.

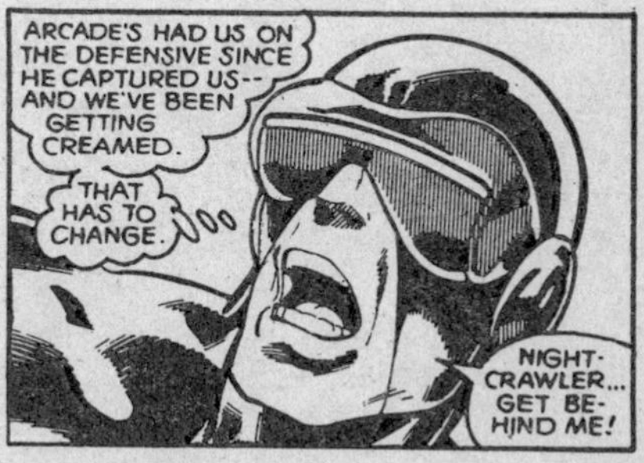
ARCADE'S HAD US ON THE DEFENSIVE SINCE HE CAPTURED US-- AND WE'VE BEEN GETTING CREAMED.
THAT HAS TO CHANGE.
NIGHT-CRAWLER... GET BE-HIND ME!

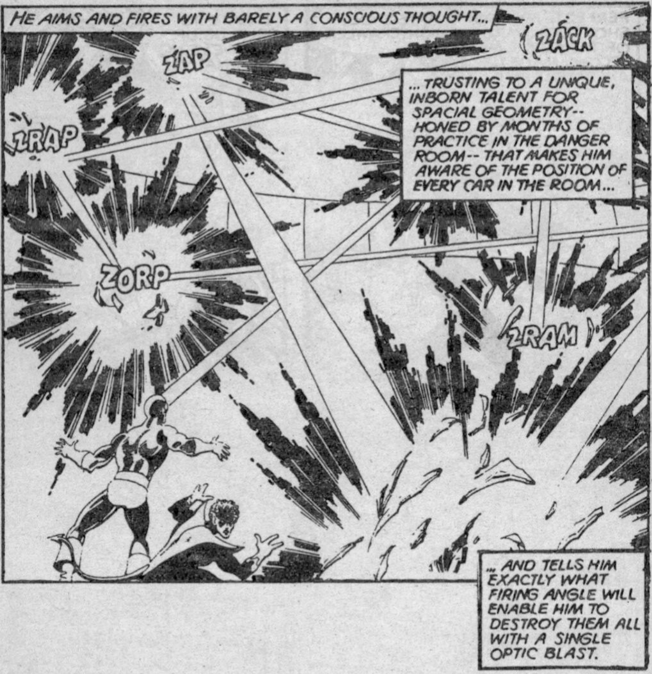
HE AIMS AND FIRES WITH BARELY A CONSCIOUS THOUGHT...
ZACK
ZAP
...TRUSTING TO A UNIQUE, INBORN TALENT FOR SPACIAL GEOMETRY-- HONED BY MONTHS OF PRACTICE IN THE DANGER ROOM-- THAT MAKES HIM AWARE OF THE POSITION OF EVERY CAR IN THE ROOM...
ZRAP
ZORP
ZRAM
...AND TELLS HIM EXACTLY WHAT FIRING ANGLE WILL ENABLE HIM TO DESTROY THEM ALL WITH A SINGLE OPTIC BLAST.

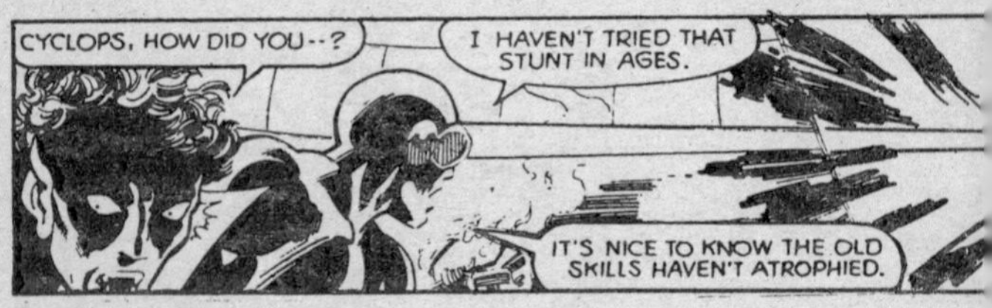
CYCLOPS, HOW DID YOU--?
I HAVEN'T TRIED THAT STUNT IN AGES.
IT'S NICE TO KNOW THE OLD SKILLS HAVEN'T ATROPHIED.

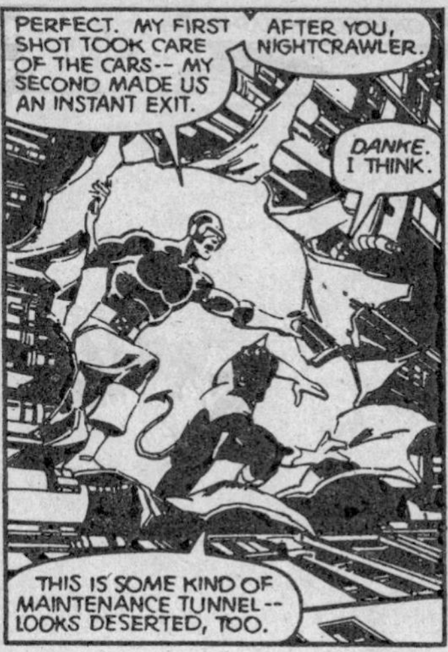
PERFECT. MY FIRST SHOT TOOK CARE OF THE CARS-- MY SECOND MADE US AN INSTANT EXIT.
AFTER YOU, NIGHTCRAWLER.
DANKE. I THINK.
THIS IS SOME KIND OF MAINTENANCE TUNNEL-- LOOKS DESERTED, TOO.

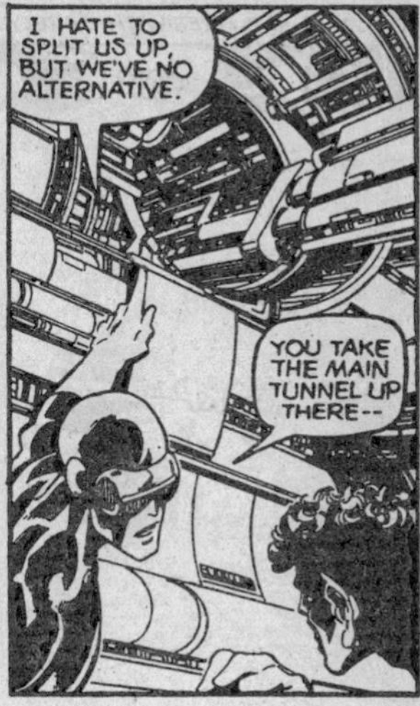
I HATE TO SPLIT US UP, BUT WE'VE NO ALTERNATIVE.
YOU TAKE THE MAIN TUNNEL UP THERE--

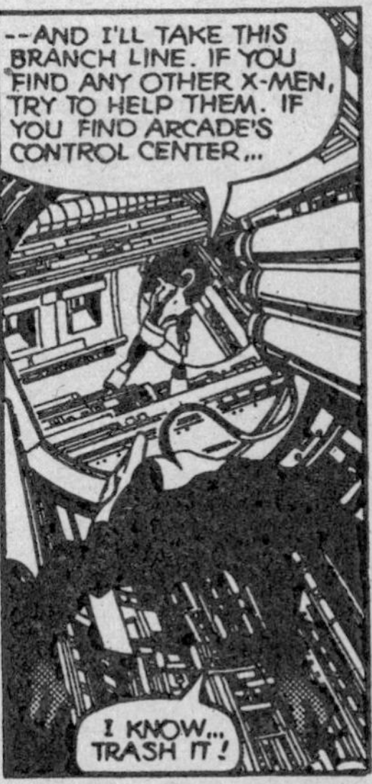
--AND I'LL TAKE THIS BRANCH LINE. IF YOU FIND ANY OTHER X-MEN, TRY TO HELP THEM. IF YOU FIND ARCADE'S CONTROL CENTER...
I KNOW... TRASH IT!

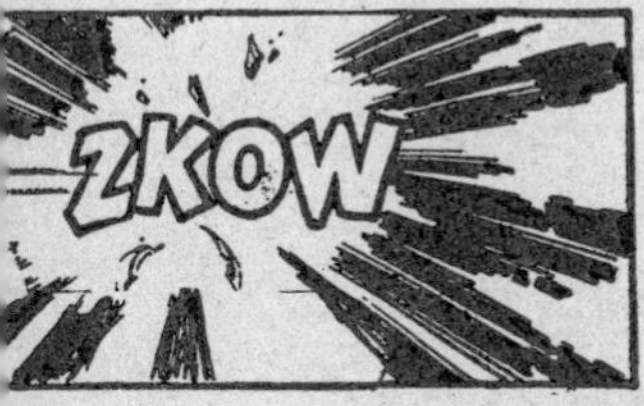
ZKOW

TROUBLE, ARCADE.

STORM'S GENERATING MORE POWER THAN THE SYSTEM CAN ABSORB. WE CAN'T HOLD HER MUCH LONGER.

YOU NEEDN'T WORRY ABOUT THE GIRLS, ARCADE. I'VE... TAKEN CARE OF THEM.

THE TUNNEL'S PROBABLY CRAMMED WITH SENSORS-- SOONER OR LATER, ARCADE'S BOUND TO FIND US.

BUT IT'S --HM?! SOUNDS LIKE A FIGHT.

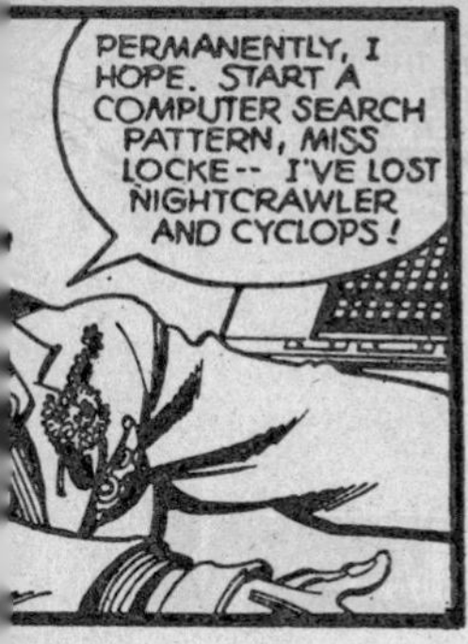
PERMANENTLY, I HOPE. START A COMPUTER SEARCH PATTERN, MISS LOCKE-- I'VE LOST NIGHTCRAWLER AND CYCLOPS!

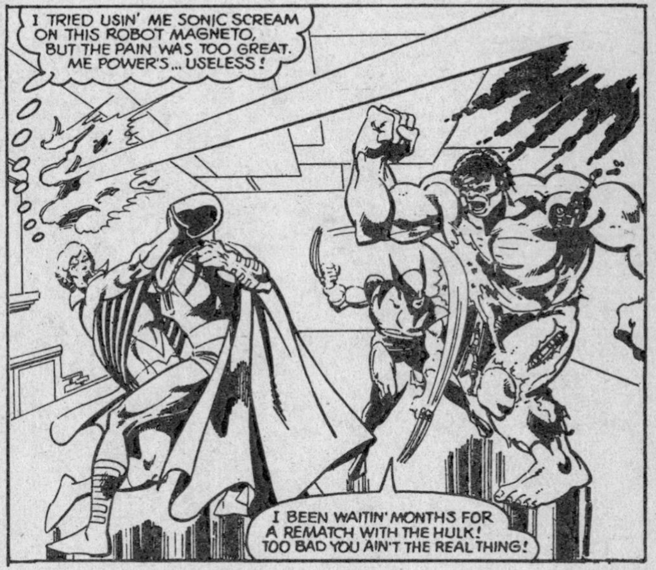
I TRIED USIN' ME SONIC SCREAM ON THIS ROBOT MAGNETO, BUT THE PAIN WAS TOO GREAT. ME POWER'S... USELESS!
I BEEN WAITIN' MONTHS FOR A REMATCH WITH THE HULK! TOO BAD YOU AIN'T THE REAL THING!

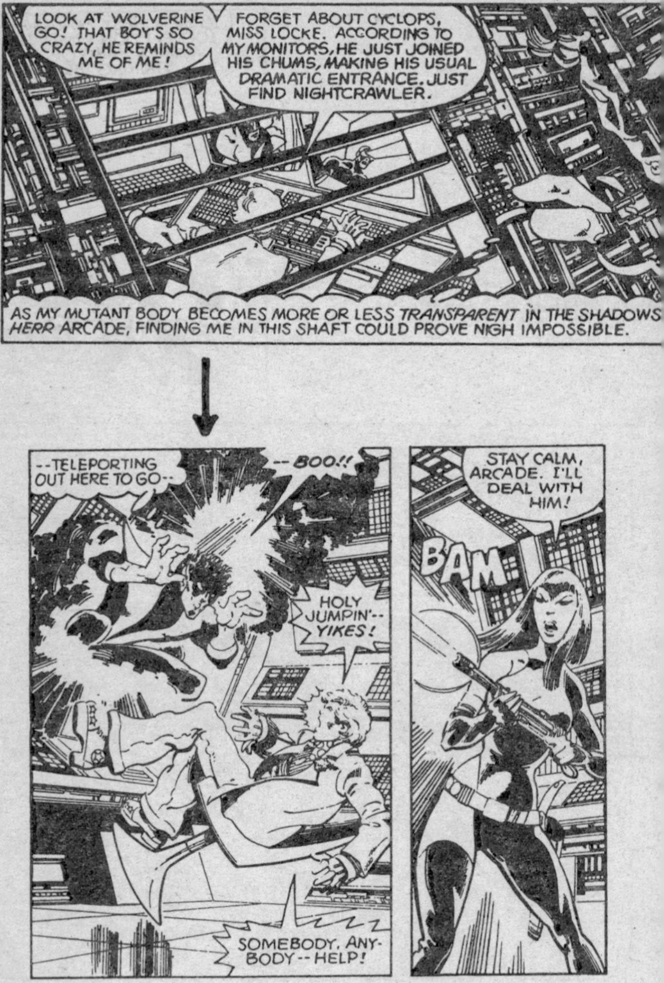
LOOK AT WOLVERINE GO! THAT BOY'S SO CRAZY, HE REMINDS ME OF ME!
FORGET ABOUT CYCLOPS, MISS LOCKE. ACCORDING TO MY MONITORS, HE JUST JOINED HIS CHUMS, MAKING HIS USUAL DRAMATIC ENTRANCE. JUST FIND NIGHTCRAWLER.
AS MY MUTANT BODY BECOMES MORE OR LESS TRANSPARENT IN THE SHADOWS HERR ARCADE, FINDING ME IN THIS SHAFT COULD PROVE NIGH IMPOSSIBLE.
--TELEPORTING OUT HERE TO GO--
--BOO!!
HOLY JUMPIN'--YIKES!
SOMEBODY. ANY-BODY--HELP!
STAY CALM, ARCADE. I'LL DEAL WITH HIM!
BAM

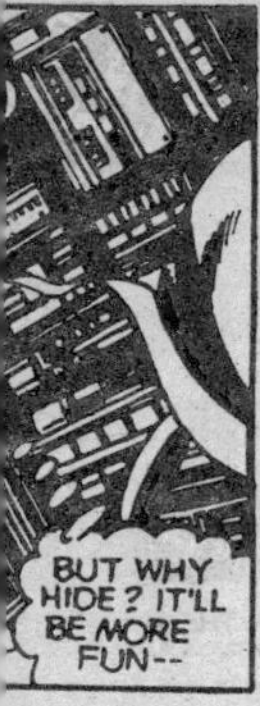
BUT WHY HIDE? IT'LL BE MORE FUN--

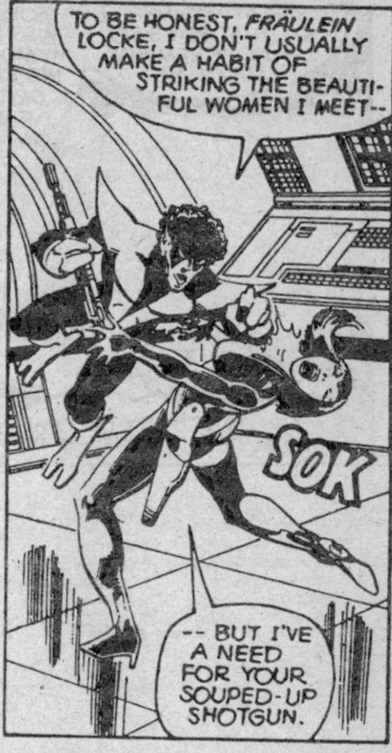
TO BE HONEST, FRÄULEIN LOCKE, I DON'T USUALLY MAKE A HABIT OF STRIKING THE BEAUTIFUL WOMEN I MEET--
SOK
-- BUT I'VE A NEED FOR YOUR SOUPED-UP SHOTGUN.

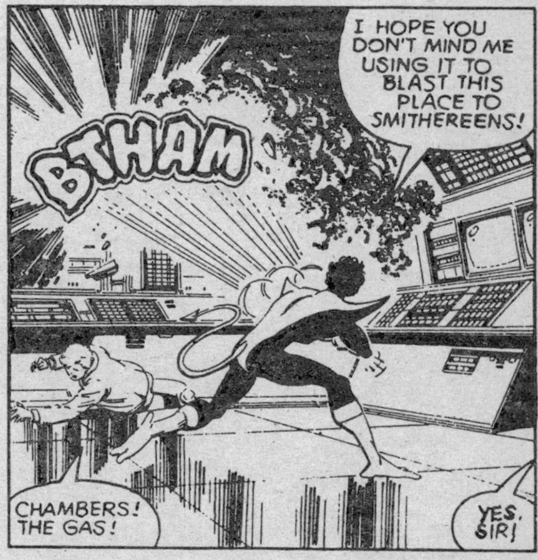
I HOPE YOU DON'T MIND ME USING IT TO BLAST THIS PLACE TO SMITHEREENS!
BTHAM
CHAMBERS! THE GAS!
YES, SIR!

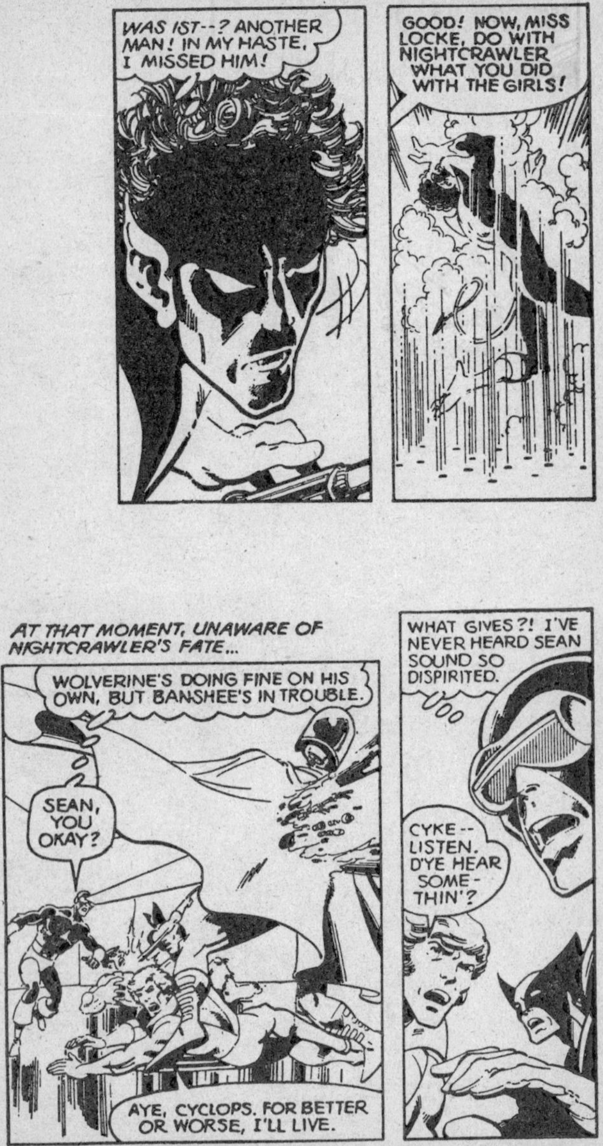
WAS IST--? ANOTHER MAN! IN MY HASTE, I MISSED HIM!
GOOD! NOW, MISS LOCKE, DO WITH NIGHTCRAWLER WHAT YOU DID WITH THE GIRLS!
AT THAT MOMENT, UNAWARE OF NIGHTCRAWLER'S FATE...
WOLVERINE'S DOING FINE ON HIS OWN, BUT BANSHEE'S IN TROUBLE.
SEAN, YOU OKAY?
AYE, CYCLOPS. FOR BETTER OR WORSE, I'LL LIVE.
WHAT GIVES?! I'VE NEVER HEARD SEAN SOUND SO DISPIRITED.
CYKE-- LISTEN. D'YE HEAR SOME-THIN'?

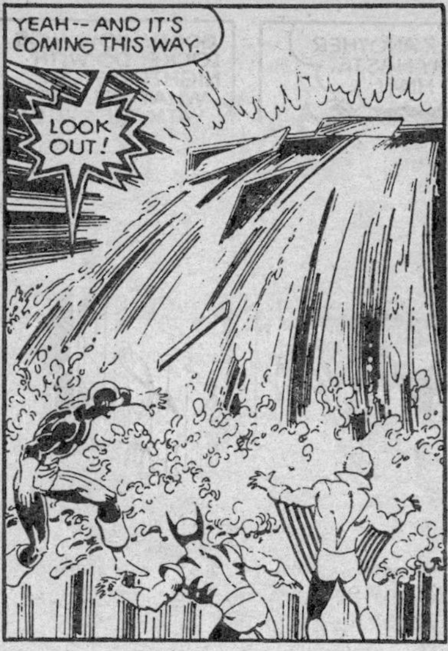
YEAH -- AND IT'S COMING THIS WAY.
LOOK OUT!

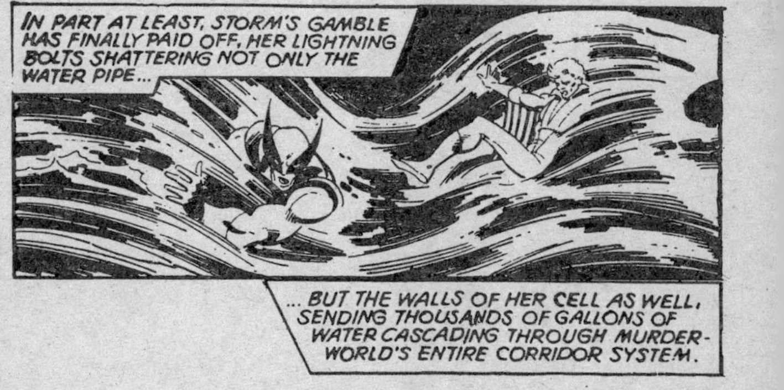
IN PART AT LEAST, STORM'S GAMBLE HAS FINALLY PAID OFF, HER LIGHTNING BOLTS SHATTERING NOT ONLY THE WATER PIPE...
...BUT THE WALLS OF HER CELL AS WELL, SENDING THOUSANDS OF GALLONS OF WATER CASCADING THROUGH MURDER-WORLD'S ENTIRE CORRIDOR SYSTEM.

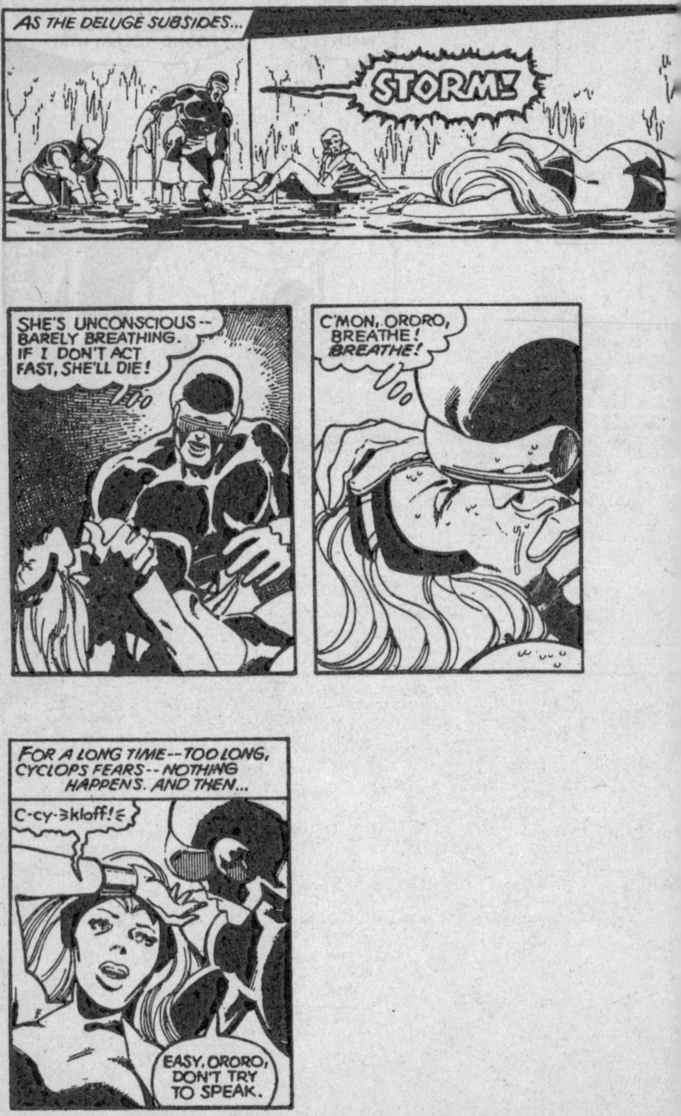
AS THE DELUGE SUBSIDES...
STORM!
SHE'S UNCONSCIOUS--BARELY BREATHING. IF I DON'T ACT FAST, SHE'LL DIE!
C'MON, ORORO, BREATHE! BREATHE!
FOR A LONG TIME--TOO LONG, CYCLOPS FEARS--NOTHING HAPPENS. AND THEN...
C-cy-kloff!
EASY, ORORO, DON'T TRY TO SPEAK.

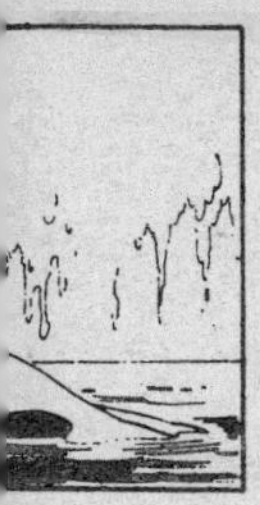

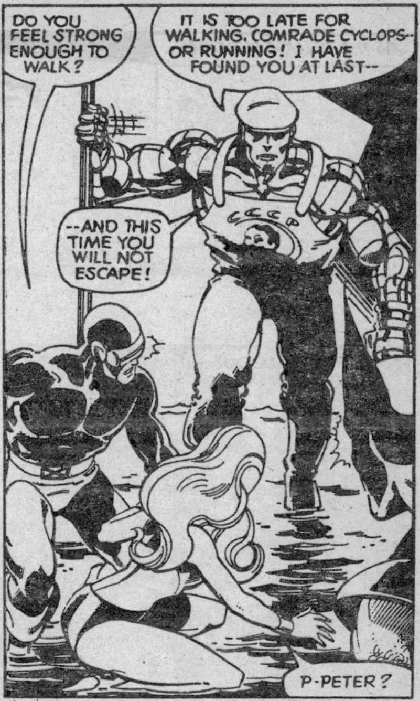

DO YOU FEEL STRONG ENOUGH TO WALK?
IT IS TOO LATE FOR WALKING, COMRADE CYCLOPS--OR RUNNING! I HAVE FOUND YOU AT LAST--
--AND THIS TIME YOU WILL NOT ESCAPE!
CCCP
P-PETER?

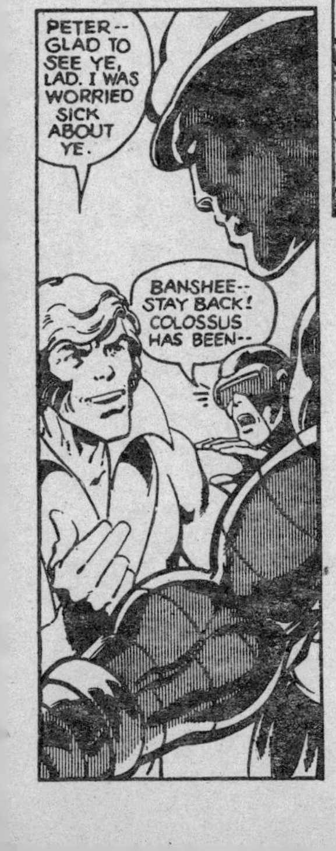

PETER--GLAD TO SEE YE, LAD. I WAS WORRIED SICK ABOUT YE.
BANSHEE--STAY BACK! COLOSSUS HAS BEEN--

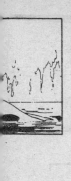

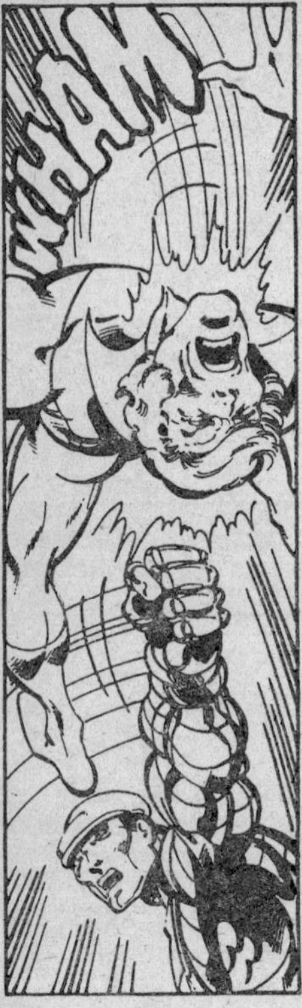
WHAM

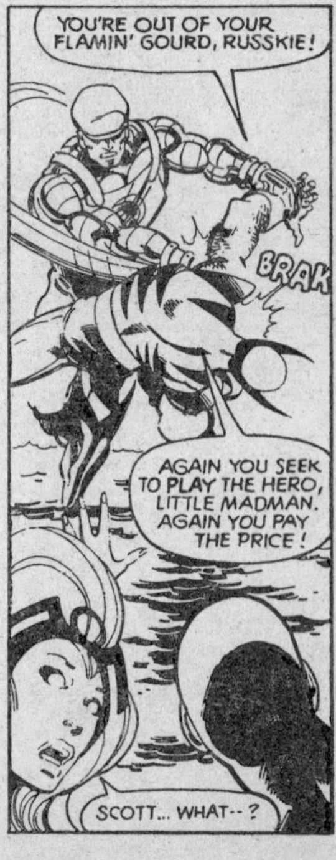
YOU'RE OUT OF YOUR FLAMIN' GOURD, RUSSKIE!
BRAK
AGAIN YOU SEEK TO PLAY THE HERO, LITTLE MADMAN. AGAIN YOU PAY THE PRICE!
SCOTT... WHAT-- ?

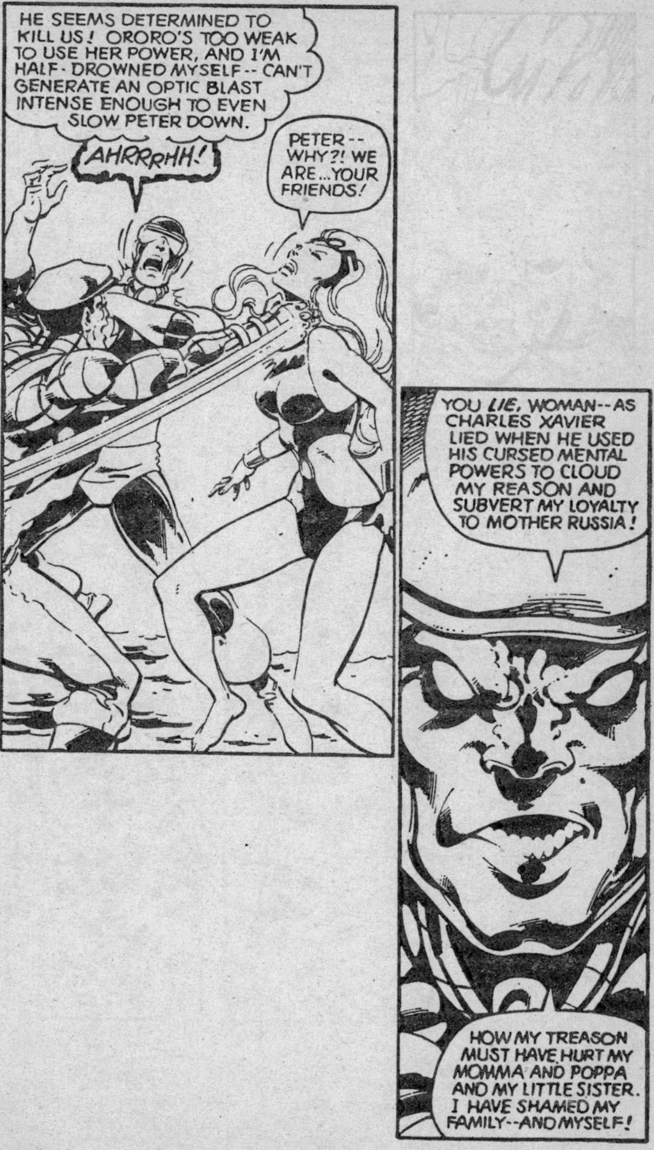
HE SEEMS DETERMINED TO KILL US! ORORO'S TOO WEAK TO USE HER POWER, AND I'M HALF-DROWNED MYSELF-- CAN'T GENERATE AN OPTIC BLAST INTENSE ENOUGH TO EVEN SLOW PETER DOWN.
AHRRRHH!
PETER-- WHY?! WE ARE...YOUR FRIENDS!
YOU *LIE*, WOMAN--AS CHARLES XAVIER LIED WHEN HE USED HIS CURSED MENTAL POWERS TO CLOUD MY REASON AND SUBVERT MY LOYALTY TO MOTHER RUSSIA!
HOW MY TREASON MUST HAVE HURT MY MOMMA AND POPPA AND MY LITTLE SISTER. I HAVE SHAMED MY FAMILY--AND MYSELF!

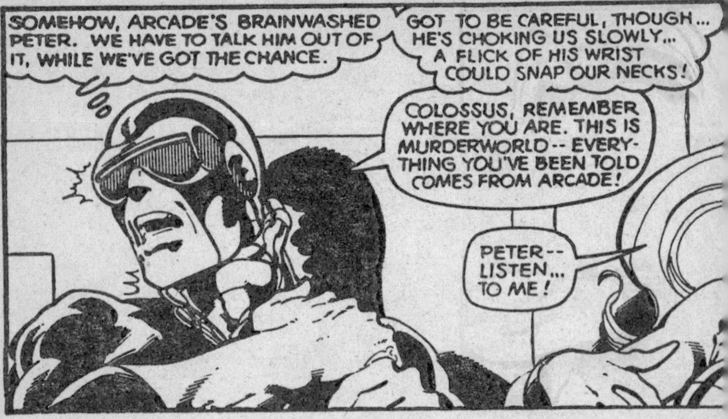
SOMEHOW, ARCADE'S BRAINWASHED PETER. WE HAVE TO TALK HIM OUT OF IT, WHILE WE'VE GOT THE CHANCE.
GOT TO BE CAREFUL, THOUGH... HE'S CHOKING US SLOWLY... A FLICK OF HIS WRIST COULD SNAP OUR NECKS!
COLOSSUS, REMEMBER WHERE YOU ARE. THIS IS MURDERWORLD -- EVERY-THING YOU'VE BEEN TOLD COMES FROM ARCADE!
PETER-- LISTEN... TO ME!

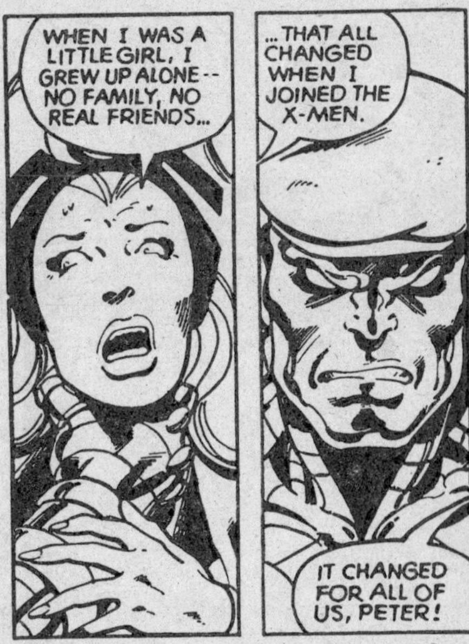
WHEN I WAS A LITTLE GIRL, I GREW UP ALONE-- NO FAMILY, NO REAL FRIENDS...
...THAT ALL CHANGED WHEN I JOINED THE X-MEN.
IT CHANGED FOR ALL OF US, PETER!

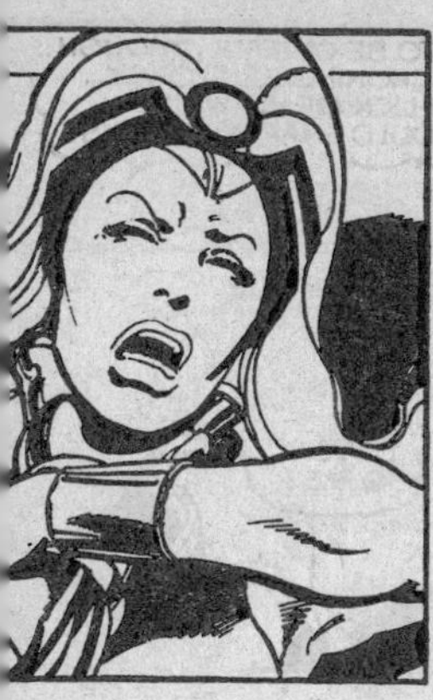

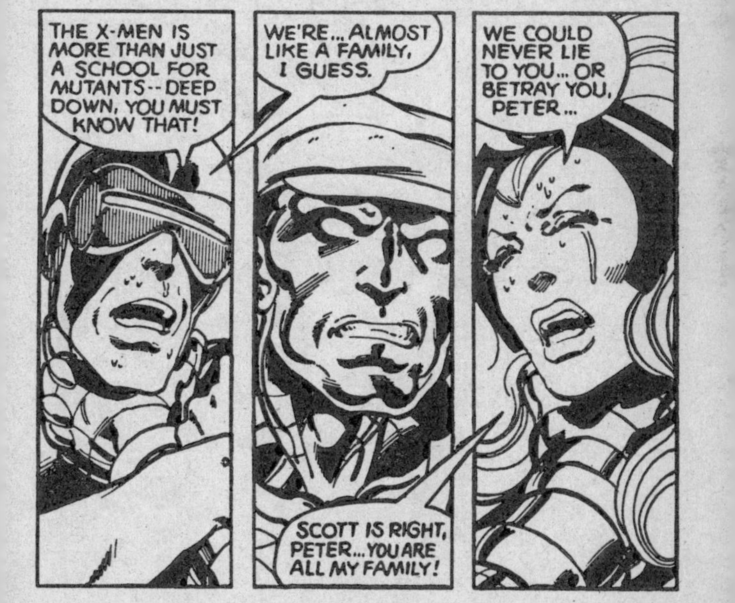
THE X-MEN IS MORE THAN JUST A SCHOOL FOR MUTANTS--DEEP DOWN, YOU MUST KNOW THAT!
WE'RE... ALMOST LIKE A FAMILY, I GUESS.
SCOTT IS RIGHT, PETER... YOU ARE ALL MY FAMILY!
WE COULD NEVER LIE TO YOU... OR BETRAY YOU, PETER...

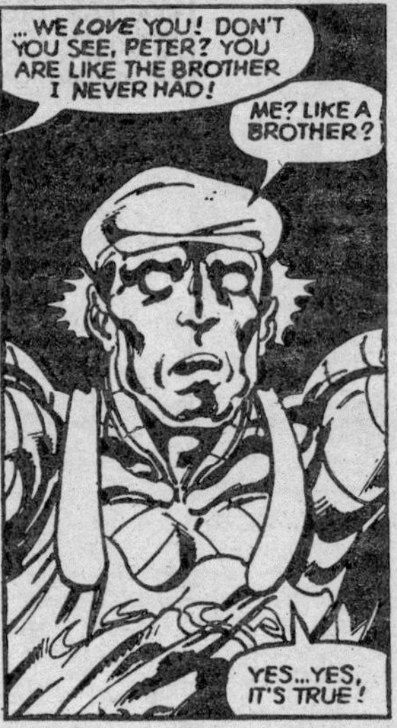
...WE LOVE YOU! DON'T YOU SEE, PETER? YOU ARE LIKE THE BROTHER I NEVER HAD!
ME? LIKE A BROTHER?
YES...YES, IT'S TRUE!

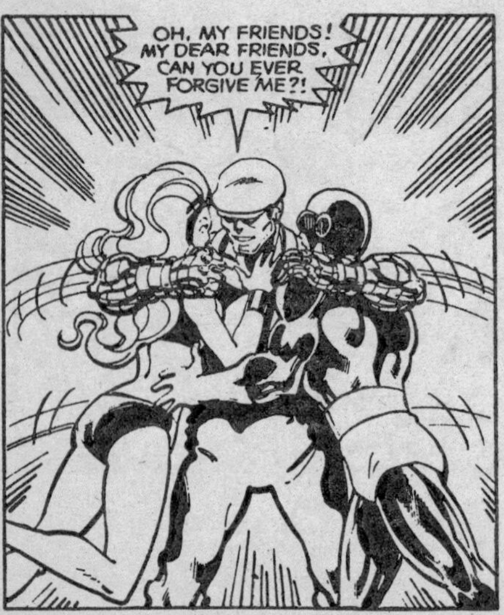
OH, MY FRIENDS! MY DEAR FRIENDS, CAN YOU EVER FORGIVE ME?!

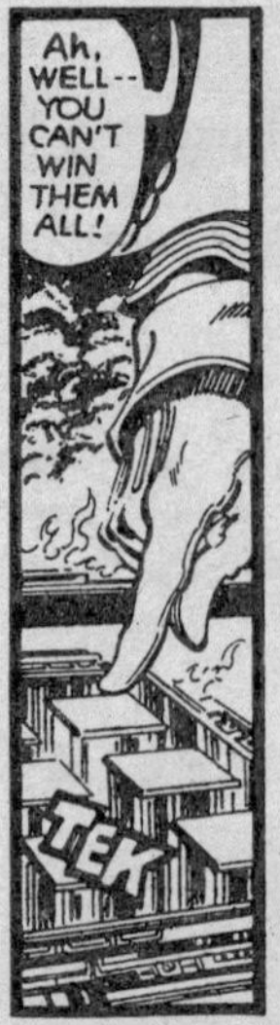
Ah, WELL-- YOU CAN'T WIN THEM ALL!
TEK

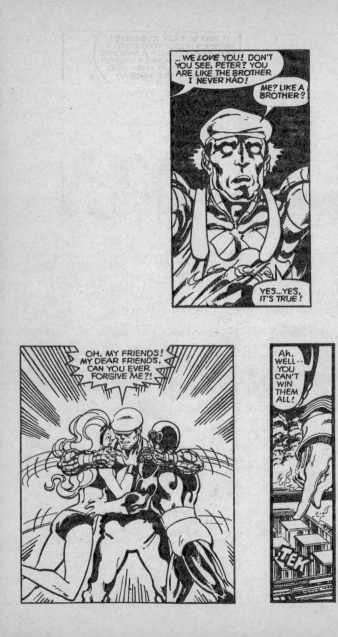

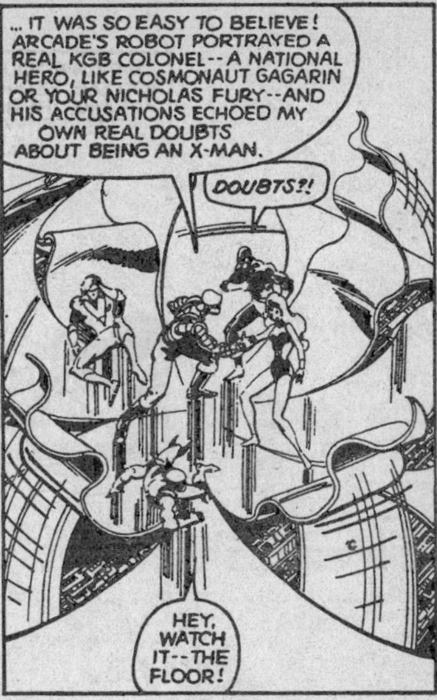
... IT WAS SO EASY TO BELIEVE! ARCADE'S ROBOT PORTRAYED A REAL KGB COLONEL--A NATIONAL HERO, LIKE COSMONAUT GAGARIN OR YOUR NICHOLAS FURY--AND HIS ACCUSATIONS ECHOED MY OWN REAL DOUBTS ABOUT BEING AN X-MAN.
DOUBTS?!
HEY, WATCH IT--THE FLOOR!

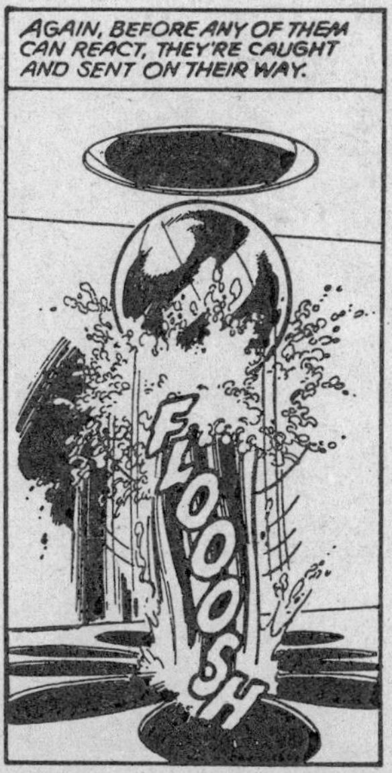
AGAIN, BEFORE ANY OF THEM CAN REACT, THEY'RE CAUGHT AND SENT ON THEIR WAY.
FLOOOOSH

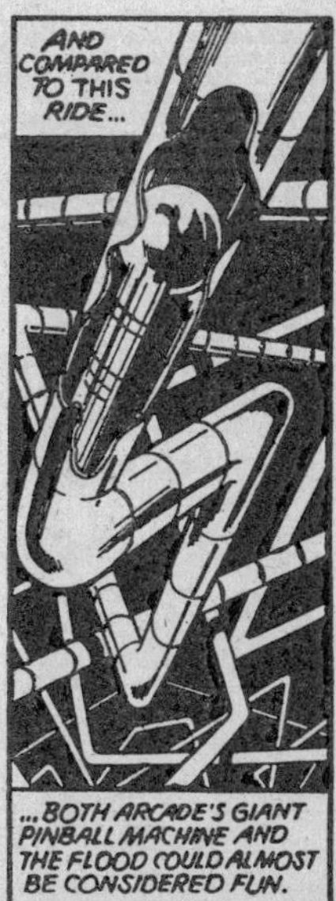
AND COMPARED TO THIS RIDE...
...BOTH ARCADE'S GIANT PINBALL MACHINE AND THE FLOOD COULD ALMOST BE CONSIDERED FUN.

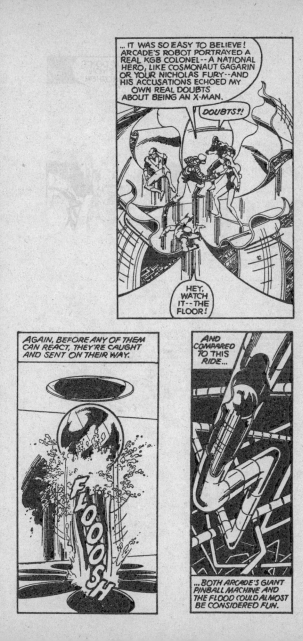

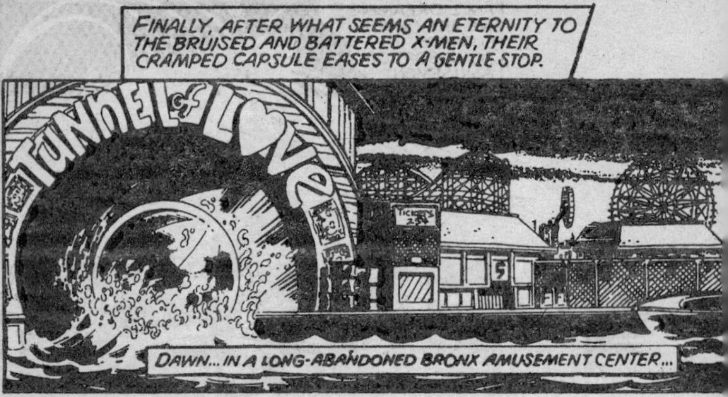
FINALLY, AFTER WHAT SEEMS AN ETERNITY TO THE BRUISED AND BATTERED X-MEN, THEIR CRAMPED CAPSULE EASES TO A GENTLE STOP.
TUNNEL of LOVE
DAWN... IN A LONG-ABANDONED BRONX AMUSEMENT CENTER...

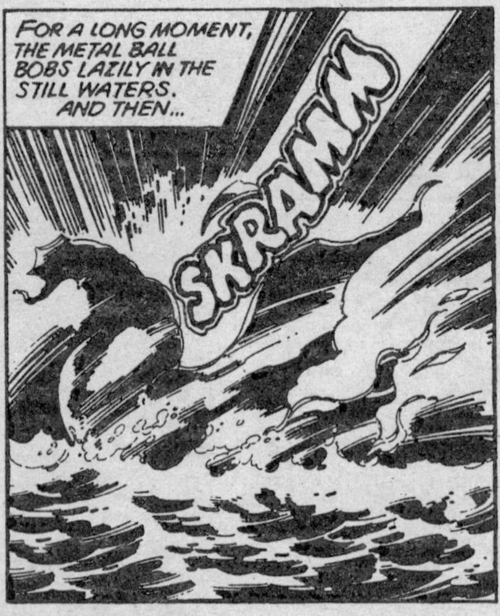
FOR A LONG MOMENT, THE METAL BALL BOBS LAZILY IN THE STILL WATERS. AND THEN...
SKRAMM

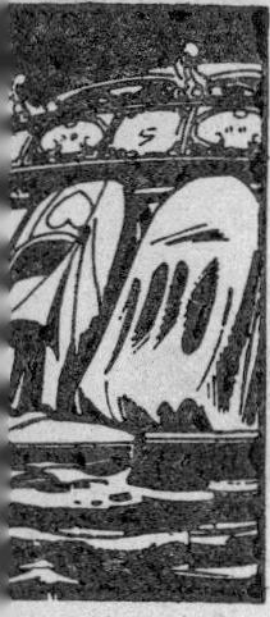

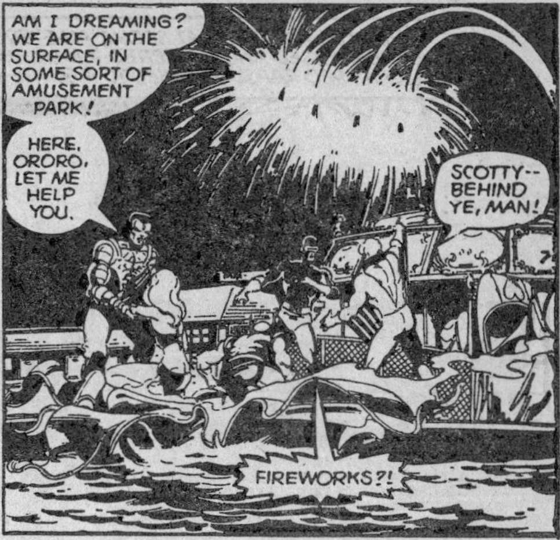
AM I DREAMING? WE ARE ON THE SURFACE, IN SOME SORT OF AMUSEMENT PARK!
HERE, ORORO, LET ME HELP YOU.
SCOTTY-- BEHIND YE, MAN!
FIREWORKS?!

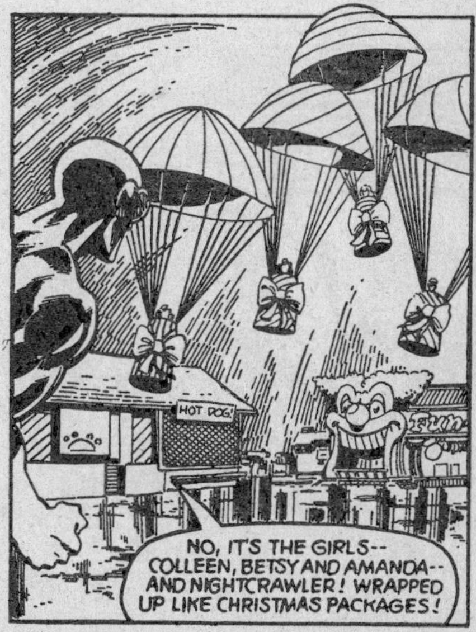
HOT DOG!
NO, IT'S THE GIRLS-- COLLEEN, BETSY AND AMANDA-- AND NIGHTCRAWLER! WRAPPED UP LIKE CHRISTMAS PACKAGES!

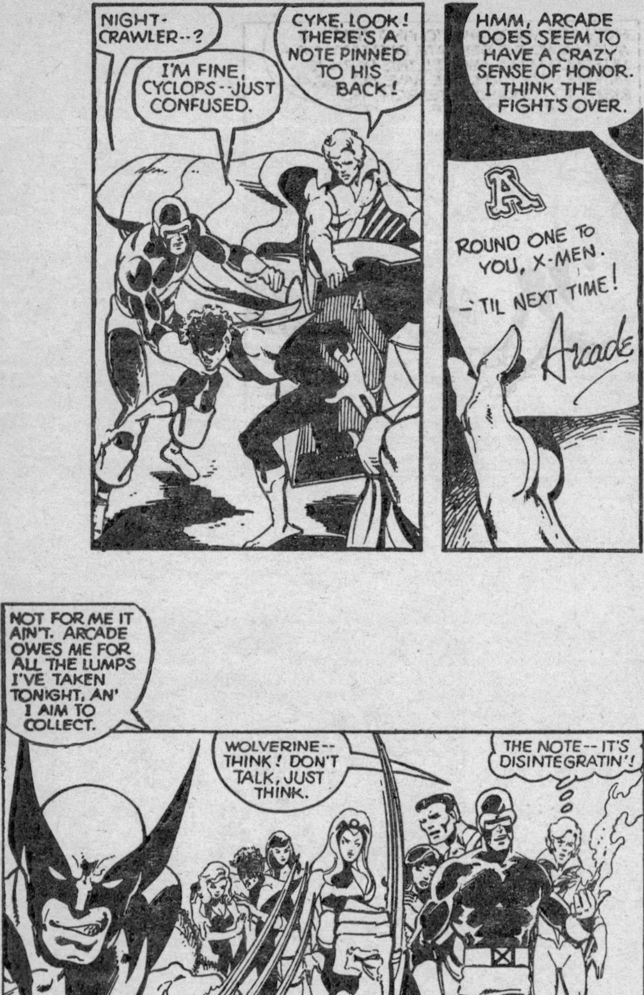
NIGHT-CRAWLER--?
I'M FINE, CYCLOPS--JUST CONFUSED.
CYKE, LOOK! THERE'S A NOTE PINNED TO HIS BACK!
HMM, ARCADE DOES SEEM TO HAVE A CRAZY SENSE OF HONOR. I THINK THE FIGHT'S OVER.
A
ROUND ONE TO YOU, X-MEN.
-'TIL NEXT TIME!
Arcade
NOT FOR ME IT AIN'T. ARCADE OWES ME FOR ALL THE LUMPS I'VE TAKEN TONIGHT, AN' I AIM TO COLLECT.
WOLVERINE--THINK! DON'T TALK, JUST THINK.
THE NOTE--IT'S DISINTEGRATIN'!

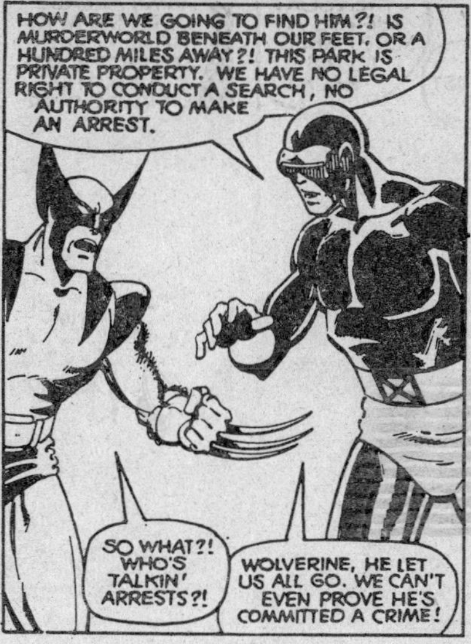
HOW ARE WE GOING TO FIND HIM?! IS MURDERWORLD BENEATH OUR FEET, OR A HUNDRED MILES AWAY?! THIS PARK IS PRIVATE PROPERTY. WE HAVE NO LEGAL RIGHT TO CONDUCT A SEARCH, NO AUTHORITY TO MAKE AN ARREST.
SO WHAT?! WHO'S TALKIN' ARRESTS?!
WOLVERINE, HE LET US ALL GO. WE CAN'T EVEN PROVE HE'S COMMITTED A CRIME!

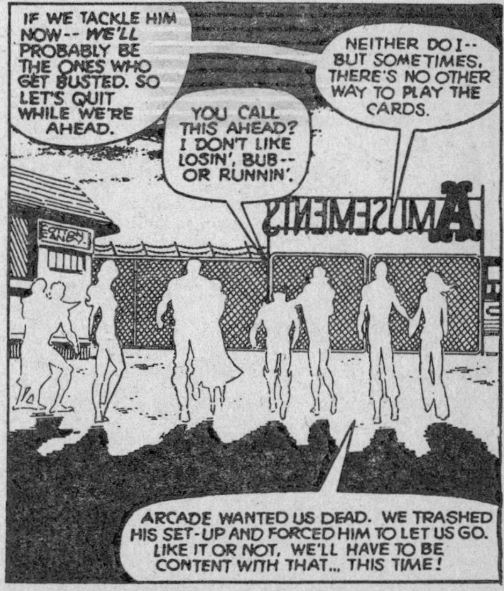
IF WE TACKLE HIM NOW-- WE'LL PROBABLY BE THE ONES WHO GET BUSTED. SO LET'S QUIT WHILE WE'RE AHEAD.
YOU CALL THIS AHEAD? I DON'T LIKE LOSIN', BUB-- OR RUNNIN'.
NEITHER DO I-- BUT SOMETIMES, THERE'S NO OTHER WAY TO PLAY THE CARDS.
ARCADE WANTED US DEAD. WE TRASHED HIS SET-UP AND FORCED HIM TO LET US GO. LIKE IT OR NOT, WE'LL HAVE TO BE CONTENT WITH THAT... THIS TIME!